MANAGED CARE
An Agency Guide to Surviving and Thriving

BY

DAVID EMENHISER
ROBERT BARKER
MADELYN DEWOODY

CHILD WELFARE LEAGUE OF AMERICA · WASHINGTON, DC

CHILD WELFARE LEAGUE OF AMERICA, INC.
440 First Street, NW, Suite 310, Washington, DC 20001-2085

CURRENT PRINTING (last digit)
10 9 8 7 6 5 4 3 2 1

Cover design by Paul Butler
Text design by Eve Malakoff-Klein

Printed in the United States of America

ISBN # 0-87868-597-9

CONTENTS

ACKNOWLEDGMENTS

My thanks to Nickola Dixon, who prepared all the working drafts of my assigned chapters for me.
—M.D.W.

My thanks to Charlene Coates, who devoted a number of hours to word processing; my family, including my son, Gary T. Barker, who assisted in editing; and the Board of Directors of DePelchin Children's Center, who have provided me with the opportunity to gain experience in managed care and spend the time writing.
—R.B.

The trustees and the management team of St. Joseph Children's Treatment Center have been supportive of and essential to this effort. In particular, my thanks go to Tony Sculimbrene, Board President; to Anna Horn, Executive Secretary, for her work on the manuscript; and to Fred Sinay, Director of Managed Care Planning and Implementation, for his background research. I also want to thank my family for their patience during the writing process.
—D.E.

PREFACE

At CWLA's 1994 annual conference, Bob Barker and I had the opportunity to serve on a discussion panel on managed care. The session drew an overflow crowd of nearly 200 agency CEOs and board members. After the panel presentations, a question and answer session centered upon the merits of managed care. While the panel members successfully presented the major tenets of managed care, one could sense the anxiety in the audience at the prospect of systemwide change. The questions and comments from the audience members seemed to divide people into three distinct groups: those who viewed managed care as inevitable; those who believed that it would destroy traditional child welfare services; and those who voiced bewilderment about the topic.

The need for a book on the issues surrounding managed care was clear. My search for coauthors with more expertise than mine on the topic ended when Bob Barker, CEO of DePelchin Children's Center, and Madelyn DeWoody, former General Counsel and Director of Child Welfare Services of CWLA, and currently the Associate Director for Planning, Training, and Evaluation at the Massachusetts Society for the Prevention of Cruelty to Children, agreed to bring their considerable knowledge to the task.

Our purpose in writing this book is to address the issues surrounding managed care, and how agency executives, staff, and boards of directors can prepare for, survive, and even prosper during the coming revolution. In short, this book is intended to take the mystery out of managed care and to quell the anxiety of executives by demonstrating the practical steps they can take to help their agencies through the transition. Furthermore, we also hope to help CEOs and their board members regain a sense of optimism about their agencies' future in a managed care environment—without minimizing the pitfalls and challenges that lie ahead.

Child welfare agency executives, management staff members, therapists, middle managers, and board members have much to gain from reading this book. Those in the ranks of public policy, state government, mental health, and other public and private human service agencies will also find this book useful.

One of the dangers inherent in writing a book about an emerging phenomenon is that future events will overtake the authors' current perspective on the topic. To counter this, we repeatedly emphasize the core issues of managed care, lend multiple perspectives to the future of child welfare, and encourage readers to take an active role in determining the future of their agencies. Whether or not managed care is ultimately viewed as a benefit to the children we serve or as a failure will in large part depend on the results of your advocacy efforts.

We hope that this book provides the tools needed for your journey into managed care.

DAVID EMENHISER, ED.D.
January, 1995

EXECUTIVE SUMMARY

One must never lose time in vainly regretting the past, nor in
complaining about the changes which cause us discomfort,
for change is the very essence of life.
—*Anatole France [1883]*

The introduction of managed care in the child welfare field is
fundamentally revolutionizing relationships among clients,
funders, and child welfare agencies. Relationships that have
generally held constant over the past 20 years are about to
change dramatically. While managed care is often viewed as the
result of health care reform initiatives, more universal forces
than that are at work. The implementation of managed care is
being driven by the computer revolution, high-tech communication systems, the consolidation of capital, and issues of
affordability and quality. These same forces are at work in other
sectors of the economy: corporate downsizing, bank consolidation, and insurance company mergers. To assume that child
welfare and children's mental health agencies will not be dramatically affected by these revolutionary changes is, at best,
wishful thinking.

Currently, the implementation of managed care is a state-by-
state phenomenon. Over time, however, it will likely become
universal. Like the aftermath of any other revolution, some of
what existed before will be swept away. Some child welfare
agencies will not survive the transition; others will survive only
as parts of other organizations. The managed care revolution
differs from past innovations—deinstitutionalization, permanency planning, and family preservation—that largely resulted
from internal efforts to reform the field. This revolution is being
driven by external forces. In this sense, it is comparable to the

racial and religious integration that most agencies experienced in the 1960s. Few current child welfare agency executives have experienced this kind of climatic change.

The good news is that, like all revolutions, this one will create a number of opportunities for agencies. For those agencies that prepare for and decide to embrace the new reality, a host of possibilities will emerge, including the opportunity to implement new approaches to serving children, explore new funding sources, reorganize, and build new partnerships.

This executive summary is not a substitute for the entire text, especially considering the technical and in-depth nature of the topic, but a sampler to whet the appetite of those agencies preparing for managed care.

Chapter 1: The Basics

While managed care appears to be a new phenomenon, its roots can be traced back to 1929. In that year, teachers in Dallas, Texas, joined an organization (through Baylor College of Medicine) to cover the costs of hospitalization for the group. Over time, managed care has become the predominant form of private health care delivery and financing. On the public side, it is becoming a force in the provision of health care, mental health care, and social services as state officials seek to control Medicaid and other government expenditures.

What is Managed Care?

Three major activities characterize managed care systems: (1) arrangement for the delivery of services, (2) review of the quality and appropriateness of the services provided, and (3) reimbursement of providers who deliver services. These activities are tied to the two major goals of managed care: (1) reducing the overall costs of service delivery, and (2) ensuring the quality of services that are delivered. Costs are addressed by limiting reimbursements for service and by controlling inappropriate service use through reviews of the intensity of services and their duration. Managed care plans also focus on shifting reimbursement from a fee-for-service orientation to one where service providers share the financial risk. To ensure quality, managed care organizations (MCOs) employ an array of local and national quality standards. MCOs achieve quality care by negotiating with their providers, assessing customer satisfaction, and establishing outcome measures and procedures for continuous quality improvement.

Elements of Managed Care

While managed care may take a variety of forms, all plans have certain common elements. Each consumer is "enrolled" in the plan and agrees to its terms. Managed care plans establish networks of service providers, who agree to the terms of a contract. These providers are selected based upon the quality, cost, and range of services they provide. Clients usually access the plan through a single point of entry—a primary care provider who serves as a gatekeeper and manages client access to specialists and other plan service providers.

In addition, managed care companies use a variety of reimbursement systems designed to shift the financial risk to service providers and to control the cost of services. One approach is a capitation contract, which prepays the service provider a set monthly amount for each individual enrolled in the plan, in return for the provider's agreement to provide a range of services for that set amount. Other payment methods include discounted rates, fee schedules, and the traditional (but relatively less popular) fee-for-service plan. As mentioned above, managed care places great emphasis on continuing quality assurance and improvement, and on utilization review programs.

Managed care plans encourage enrollees to use member service providers by allowing enrollees to obtain services with little or no copayment inside the managed care network, and by requiring significantly higher copayments from enrollees who use providers outside of the plan. While managed care often take the form of health maintenance organizations (HMOs), there are a number of other forms, which offer a range of services and provide services through different types of contractual arrangements. Appendix A provides a glossary of the most common managed care concepts.

Managed Care and Mental Health Care Services

Most managed care companies offer some form of mental health coverage for their enrollees. The costs of mental health care, however, have been more difficult to control than those of physical health care, due to the subjective nature of mental health care, the lack of a single standard of care and treatment, and the variety of practitioners and treatment modalities. Managed care systems tend to limit their clients' use of mental health services by requiring a physician's referral and out-of-pocket payments for a percentage of the costs, and by restricting the number of sessions or dollar amounts covered. The trends in behavioral health care include payer/MCO-driven decision making as to the effectiveness and efficiency of the service, outcome measurement, and consumer sensitivity.

Managed Care and Medicaid

With rising competition in the private insurance market, MCOs are becoming increasingly important in the realm of public insurance programs, especially Medicaid. Under current Medicaid law, five major types of managed care are permitted: (1) voluntary participation of Medicaid beneficiaries in HMOs; (2) use of targeted case-management services included in the state Medicaid plans as an optional service; (3) state plan exceptions that allow voluntary capitated service delivery programs; (4) freedom-of-choice waivers that permit states to require Medicaid-eligible individuals to receive services through a managed care, capitated program; and (5) waivers under §1115(a) of the Social Security Act that allow states to use managed care as a Medicaid "research and demonstration" program. The fifth option—§1115(a) waivers—has generated most of the attention recently as states have used it to reform their health care systems and contain costs. Section 1115(a) waivers provide states with considerable flexibility in establishing their own eligibility rules, service coverage, and provider arrangements. In those states that have received §1115(a) waivers, some themes are evident, such as eligibility expansion, the use of cost sharing with consumers and risk sharing with service providers, and increased managed care enrollment. A number of questions have been raised by such innovative application of waivers, including concerns that shifting financial risks to service providers may actually create a disincentive to serve, and that clinical decisions are being influenced by cost.

Implications for Child Welfare Agencies

Child welfare agencies in states that are moving toward adopting a managed care system must not hesitate to address a number of practical and strategic issues. The inclusion of special-needs populations in managed health care plans offers a number of advantages for clients and agencies, including expansions in early diagnosis and treatment, increased flexibility in treatment, and new sources of funding for community-based services such as wraparound. Managed care also poses risks, however, especially for children with the most intensive service needs, who require comprehensive, long-term, and often expensive treatment, and whose placements in care are often quite transient. Child welfare agencies must ready themselves by analyzing how the goals of managed care can be met within the framework of their agencies' mission, creating compatible services and pricing structures, and comprehending legal issues regarding contracts and liability. It is during this interim period that child welfare agencies have both an opportunity and an obligation to work with MCOs to insure that the special and complex needs of their agencies' clients are met through this new system of care and treatment.

Chapter 2: Preparation and Positioning

Chapter 2's topics are most relevant to executives, staff members, and board members of agencies that are nearing the point of transition from a fee-for-service to a managed care environment. During this transition, the very survival of the agency is at stake. Agencies must begin now to prepare their leadership, programs, finances, and marketing efforts for this new climate. Chapter 2 presents a number of offensive and defensive strategies to guide agencies through the dangers of the conversion period.

Leadership

The first and most important step in preparing for managed care is to ready the agency's leadership for change. During times of crisis, those who inhabit organizations tend to close ranks behind their leader and become more dependent than ever before upon that person's guidance.

At this initial stage, CEOs need to educate themselves about managed care and assess their level of comfort with change. Simultaneously, they need to educate their management team members and boards of directors about the concepts of managed care. With this preparation as a base, they can begin to strengthen their boards by selecting new members with the needed expertise, add managed care goals to their agencies' strategic plans, and intensify their advocacy efforts to guide their states' managed care plans and their implementation.

Furthermore, leaders must realize the power of self-fulfilling prophecies, and how contagious positive or negative attitudes about the future are with staff and board members. Leaders are entrusted with inordinate power to model and communicate their visions of the future to their organizations. The ability of an organization to survive and thrive in this new environment might well be decided by its leader's attitude and perspective.

Programs

Probably the most difficult aspect of an agency's conversion to a managed care environment will be changing its mix of programs. Managed care will emphasize prevention and early intervention, will erect barriers to placing children in expensive out-of-home care settings, and will limit lengths of stay. Therapists and middle managers will experience the greatest stress during the transition because they must fundamentally change their orientation to service provision, therapeutic independence, and relationships with their clients.

Agencies can adopt a number of offensive strategies to position themselves and their programs for managed care.

1. Agencies should consider expanding their continuum of care and treatment options to offer "one-stop shopping"

for families and children in need of treatment services. MCOs will be attracted to agencies that have services available 24-hours a day, that respond quickly to a crisis, and that cover a wide geographic area, especially those that have a number of regional outpatient offices to enhance accessibility.

2. Agencies should emphasize programmatic unity and ease of client transfer to "step-down" services if they are to make a successful transition to managed care. While many agencies offer an impressive array of services, they lack programmatic and clinical unity.

3. Agencies should consider unifying and streamlining their admissions processes to speed response time, eliminate multiple points of entry, and create an agencywide admission criteria. In a behavioral care setting, agencies will not have the luxury of rejecting referrals.

4. MCOs seeking service providers will be emphasizing outcome indicators to measure the success of agency treatment programs and client surveys to assess satisfaction rates. Frankly, child welfare agencies should have been employing these methods for years, but have been slow to embrace quality assurance measures and procedures. Agencies that do not have such programs in place should implement them now if they hope to have data available during the critical phase of marketing themselves to MCOs.

Three other offensive strategies with broad implications for child welfare agencies are the implementation of computer networks, utilization review, and partnerships.

Much of the innovation demonstrated by MCOs is tied to the sophistication of their computer networks. Agencies that develop or expand their networks will be able to speed their billing processes and limit the staff time dedicated to client records, thus making themselves increasingly attractive to MCOs.

Managed care will probably lead to the demise of traditional

therapeutic independence due to the implementation of utilization review systems, best practice standards, and "brief therapy"
modalities. With a generous amount of training and guidance,
the majority of therapists will be able to make the transition.
Some, however, will not. This latter group can create an internal
challenge to an agency's transition to the new reality.

Finally, agencies and their boards should consider forming
partnerships with other organizations and networks. Such en-
deavors can strengthen an agency by teaming it with others that
provide the services it lacks (e.g., chemical dependency, adult
mental health, inpatient hospitalization, etc.), and by spreading
the financial risk of a capitated contract. Conversely, partner(s)
with a questionable commitment to quality or a weak financial
structure can be a detriment. Agencies should look for partners
who share their values and have trustworthy management.

Finances

The ability of an agency to provide services that respond to a
need, combined with the following defensive strategies, could
set the stage for a successful move toward providing behavioral
health care services in a managed care environment. Defensive
financial strategies use an agency's assets to ride out the storm
of the transitional period.

1. Internally, or with the help of an accounting firm, agen-
    cies should conduct a profit center study to discover the
    exact cost of each service, not just the rate charged. This
    knowledge is essential during negotiations with MCOs.

2. Agencies should work with their current bank (or find a new
    one, if necessary) to expand their line of credit. A line of
    credit equal to 10% to 15% of the agency's annual budget is
    probably adequate. Discussions with the bank about the line
    of credit should begin before the funds are needed.

3. In anticipation of a period of financial strain, agencies
    should prepare a reduction-in-force plan.

4. Agencies with endowments or real property assets will
    have a substantial advantage during the conversion pe-

riod. Boards, however, should be prepared for the possibility of selling unused land or dipping into the corpus of endowments as a last resort.

5. Agencies should put into place a sophisticated financial management system that provides a timely accounting of billings, accounts receivable and aging, income and expenses per program, and so forth.

6. Agencies that raise over 10% of their operational budget from private sources and apply their grant writing capability to secure local, state, and federal funds will find these efforts pay great dividends during the conversion process.

Pursuing Competitive Advantage

In the competitive environment of managed care, nonprofit child welfare/children's mental health agencies have a number of advantages over for-profit and government-sponsored providers. Nonprofit agencies have learned to provide cost-effective services that generate income, whereas public agencies are often dependent on the size of the government allocation and the taxpayers' commitment to the population they serve. Nonprofit child welfare agencies have skills and flexibility that are more in keeping with the private sector than do public sector agencies such as mental health centers.

Nonprofit agencies are familiar with the Medicaid-eligible clientele, and have long histories of serving abused or neglected children, children with emotional handicaps, and their families. Furthermore, they have mission-directed staffs that are committed to the values of quality care and treatment. These values are imbedded in the fabric of the organizations, not dictated by government regulation or motivated by the pursuit of profits.

Nonprofit agencies have a substantial advantage in that their prices are usually lower than those of government-sponsored mental health centers, and substantially below those of for-profits agencies and hospitals. Many nonprofit agencies own their facilities and have financial reserves or endowments that lower operating expenses and provide an important cushion. In addition, an important niche market in the new order will be the combination of therapeutic services and housing, a traditional strength of nonprofit agencies. While the use of out-of-home care may be limited, it will not be eliminated, as it provides a less expensive alternative to inpatient hospitalization.

Finally, nonprofit agencies have a long history of community service and visibility, resulting in a measure of credibility and legitimacy that will be attractive to MCOs and will provide an advantage over for-profit and government-sponsored service providers.

Marketing

All of an agency's preparation and positioning will be for naught unless it develops an aggressive and entrepreneurial marketing plan that establishes challenging goals, defines a geographic territory, and identifies the MCOs that it plans to approach. Agency executives and boards should use their contacts to identify prospective MCOs, then employ a market segmentation approach to identify the needs of these companies, determine how to gain access to their leadership, and devise a plan to present the agency as the solution to their needs.

Agencies can employ a number of techniques to give themselves the inside track over their competitors. These include using state agency contacts, obtaining professional advice to structure marketing plans, and exploiting the state's bidding process to identify prospects and obtain valuable market research data. Ultimately, however, the success of an agency's efforts to secure managed care contracts will hinge on the value, price, and quality of its services.

Chapter 3: Implementation

Chapter 3, the most technical section of this book, probably deserves two readings. Capitated contracts and services lie at the heart of managed care. Mastery of this topic can ease the transition of agencies to becoming behavioral health care providers under managed care.

Capitation payment models, in existence for more than a decade, were developed to give insurance companies and employers the ability to predict their health care costs for an entire year. Simply put, capitation means that an insurance company, MCO, or service provider sets a fee per member/client to deliver some or all of the services specified under a health care plan. Behavioral health care benefits are commonly provided separately from medical and surgical benefits. This separation is known as a carve-out.

In behavioral health care carve-outs, the payer (an MCO, insurance company, or employer) pays the service provider a fee per member, per month, in the range of $1.50–$5.00. Although there are almost as many payment and plan variations as there are plans, the payment rate is typically based on several factors: (1) the basic plan benefit, (2) whether the provider can collect any copayments, (3) service utilization history of plan members, and (4) the number of enrollees in the plan. Generally, the higher the number of enrollees, the lower the payment.

Sharing Risk/Sharing Gain

Many capitated contracts include quality and cost-control rewards. If the number of inpatient days of care remains below certain agreed-upon targets, but quality remains at expected levels, service providers may receive bonus payments or share in the profits of the insurance company or MCO. While at first glance lower inpatient utilization would not appear to matter to the payer (who pays a set monthly fee regardless of use), it can matter in the long run. If a service provider's inpatient utilization is too high, over time the provider will either need to ask the payer for a rate increase or will go out of business. The payer would then need to select another provider, disrupting continuity of care, especially for clients with chronic illnesses. Such disruptions are viewed negatively by MCOs.

To determine whether or not the payer's proposed capitated rate is realistic, agencies seeking to provide services should obtain utilization and cost histories of plan members, Armed with this information, service providers can then determine the number of clinical events per 1,000 enrollees (the standard measurement unit in managed care), and the projected cost depending on the form of treatment. Providers should consider building in a profit margin of 5% to 10% and a utilization increase risk factor of 15% over the previous highest level of utilization. In most situations, capitation rates are increased only once each year.

To succeed under a capitation system, agencies must have an initial intake triage service. This should be backed up with a 24-hour on-call contact person and immediate access to service. Many hospital admissions occur not out of clinical necessity, but because a crisis occurs after hours or on weekends, when an adequate system is not in place to respond. An improved crisis response system engages families in appropriate services. Though those services may include brief hospitalizations, more often than not less restrictive services will meet the client needs.

Coordinating with Other Services

Most child welfare agencies do not operate psychiatric hospitals. In order to enter into capitated contracts, they must have an affiliation or fee-for-service contract with an organization or hospital that has a treatment philosophy compatible with theirs. The most common model is for a psychiatrist or group to become associated with the child welfare agency, and to take responsibility for hospitalizing children and managing their hospital treatment. This increases the probability of continuity of treatment and philosophy.

Some MCOs require that their service contractors manage or directly provide both adult and child/adolescent services. Child welfare agencies should focus on their specialty of child and adolescent services, and have the MCO purchase services for adults directly from another provider. Frequently, however, MCOs choose to deliver their behavioral health care services via a single capitated contract. One approach agencies can take is to develop partnerships with organizations providing adult services, and jointly seek the capitated contract. Under such arrangements, one of the organizations holds the contract and subcontracts with the other. The organization holding and managing the contract receives compensation for taking the lead role, assuring contract compliance, and managing the risk.

Determining the Level of Risk

If the number of enrollees is low, capitation payment rates should be high. Capitation contracts are generally determined to be too risky if the total number of persons covered is less than 25,000. When the population to be served approaches 50,000, service providers are able to spread the risk effectively and have few peaks and valleys in service requests.

Agencies entering into contract negotiations should understand the probable negotiating positions of the MCO. It is safe to assume that MCOs are primarily interested in obtaining (1) reasonable capitation fees, (2) long-term contractual relationships, (3) service providers with sound reputations, and (4) service providers with sufficient resources to accept some financial risk. While nonprofit child welfare and children's mental health programs may have lower costs than other providers, they should not assume that they are the lowest cost provider in their market. Some for-profits with extensive outpatient capability can deliver services at a lower cost than nonprofits because they are not accredited or they pay their clinicians on a contract basis without benefits.

In their contract negotiations, agencies should consider presenting an initial capitated rate bid that is in the 75th percentile of the market, and that emphasizes their quality and capability. In some markets, competitive pricing may keep rates so low that quality services cannot be delivered. It may be in an agency's best interest to not participate in capitated contracts in such markets.

Changing the Organizational Culture

To convert successfully to a managed care environment, agency leaders and their staffs need to change their culture by providing increasingly timely and professional service. This is a prerequisite to meet the needs of insurance company staff, parents who are skilled at advocating for their children, and employers who are paying for the services. Such relationships are more typical of partnerships than the usual clinician-client relationship. Flexibility in scheduling appointments (including providing weekend and evening hours), and candor about treatment information are approaches that are more typical of nonprofit managed care than public agency contracted services.

The agency's business office personnel need to be efficient and responsive to clients. Parents in private insurance plans who receive their services from a child welfare organization will compare its business offices with those of hospitals and physicians. Fee-setting and collection procedures should be of high quality, and should convey an organizational climate that reflects concern and compassion, combined with a strong sense of business acumen. The physical plant should be maintained at a level of quality that is competitive with that of for-profit clinics and hospitals. Repairs should be completed promptly, and inpatient units should be designed and maintained to convey the high value placed on the children served and the needs of all family members. Parking availability, distance, lighting, and safety should be addressed in a customer-friendly manner.

Changing the Treatment Focus

The expression "the meter is running" clearly applies in capitated contracts. Clinical staff must learn to focus on helping children and their families identify the specific problems that are most urgent. Timelines have to be agreed upon, and parents need to be informed at intake as to what is expected from them. Capitated contracts assume that interventions will be brief and problem oriented. The administration of an agency should not enter into a capitated contract if it is not willing to adopt a brief therapy and least restrictive treatment philosophy.

Clinical staff in most nonprofit child welfare/children's mental health organizations have to accept the reality that services will have to be denied or discontinued in some cases when the insurance contract does not provide adequate coverage, even though there is need. Provider organizations may choose to provide additional services to the client on a fee-for-service basis, including a sliding fee scale, if funds are available to subsidize that care and treatment. The utilization management staff should take the lead in helping clinicians identify alternative treatment options for difficult cases.

Summary

Capitation payment models are not appropriate for many organizations because of the inherent financial risk involved, but some large, multiservice/multisite organizations and other agencies able to partner with agencies that provide complementary services may find capitation service contracts advantageous. This is especially true for child welfare organizations that have invested significantly in community-based, brief treatment services.

Chapter 4: Case Studies

Chapter 4 contains brief descriptions of eight agencies in six states that have totally or partially made the transition to the managed care system. Each description highlights the history, size, and array of services these agencies provide, outlines the key events that led to each organization's pursuit of managed care; details the process of managed care implementation; and reveals how each executive addressed issues of staff and board involvement in the conversion. Perhaps of greater importance is each executive's advice to other CEOs facing the challenge of managed care and their predictions of the future of child welfare agencies in a managed care environment.

While not every agency fits one mold, some common themes among the eight agencies that were studied emerged that may help to explain their success thus far with managed care. The budget of these agencies ranges from $7 million to $70 million, with an average approaching $10 million, which may provide the resources and economies of scale needed in the new managed care environment. The eight agencies profiled also have long histories, ranging from 80 to 145 years of existence, with the majority nearing the centennial mark. An agency that has survived the numerous revolutions in child welfare over the years might feel increased confidence in its ability to survive the next upheaval.

Without exception, these agencies offer a broad array of services, ranging from outpatient and community-based programs to residential and, in some cases, inpatient psychiatric services. Almost universally, the agencies described in Chapter 4 entered the world of managed care through a Medicaid provider contract. Most agencies experienced a gradual evolution toward providing managed care services. Almost without exception, each experienced some level of resistance from staff and trustees, with the greatest challenge coming from the ranks of therapists and residential staff. Each agency is struggling or has struggled with the customer service, utilization review, and seamless service aspects of managed care. Finally, and perhaps most importantly, all eight agencies benefited from activist leaders, who would rather create the future for their agencies than wait for the future to be dictated to them.

Those agencies that do not fit the profile outlined above can take heart, however. While there are many similarities among the eight agencies, there are also substantial differences. Each agency profile reveals a different course taken in response to the threats and opportunities of managed care. For some agencies, the initial pursuit of managed care resulted from a traumatic event, such as the potential closure of their residential program or their state's rapid implementation of managed care contracts. Some of the agencies were or have become affiliated with hospitals, while the majority independently pursued managed care. Some agencies took advantage of their board contacts to further their marketing and implementation efforts; others had less board involvement. Some of the profiled agencies negotiated capitated contracts; others pursued contract provider status with a number of MCOs.

One of the most interesting dichotomies among the agency executives is the range of opinions about the future impact of managed care on child welfare agencies. Those executives whose pursuit of managed care resulted from their own search for additional funding sources and new ways of enhancing quality tend to be optimistic about the future of child welfare under managed care. Those executives who reside in states where government officials are initiating managed care to contain costs tend to question the state and MCO commitment to providing quality and are concerned about the future of child welfare agencies.

Agency executives tend to like control—when the locus of control is beyond their influence, they become concerned about the motives of those who have the power to dictate the new rules of survival. Despite their standing on the optimism/pessimism scale, all eight executives view a managed care environment as inevitable.

Chapter 5: The Future

Given that managed care is a rapidly approaching reality, what does the future hold for child welfare agencies in a managed care environment? What are some of the emerging issues that executives and boards must address?

One of the key issues is the survivability of child welfare agencies, given their current organizational structure and programmatic focus. While there is certainly a threat to the future viability of organizations, a number of opportunities also exist for agencies to make substantial and positive changes. For an analogy, agencies might look to the U.S. auto industry, which has radically altered how it conducts business in order to survive foreign competition and customer demands for quality. While MCOs will, in the near term, emphasize low-cost services and interventions, over time, the emphasis will shift to quality and customer satisfaction.

Two other key points are offered: the need to invest in prevention and intervention services, and the danger presented to the child welfare field by the lack of research to support claims of programmatic success.

The Impact on Child Welfare Agencies

As managed care continues to evolve and becomes the predominant service delivery model, child welfare agencies can anticipate a range of challenges as they plan for the future. These challenges will include shifts in service delivery philosophies; increased emphasis on prevention and early intervention services; growing competition from for-profits; integration and collaboration of resources and services; changes in the accessibility, availability, and array of services; heightened accountability; emphasis on value; creation of sound management information systems; and creation of financial and cost analysis capabilities.

Opportunities to Redesign Organizations

Agency CEOs will have the opportunity to use the unique challenges of managed care to redesign the basic structure of their organizations. These opportunities include a new emphasis on data collection and outcome measures, and the communication of these findings to payers. Managed care will also lead to the reassessment of agency services, particularly those that are the most restrictive and expensive. In particular, the agency's system of judging therapeutic productivity and the conditions of employment for therapists may undergo substantial change. Usually, therapists are paid for their full-time availability, not their productivity. Suggestions are made in Chapter 5 on how to redeploy therapists by tying employment and reimbursement to agency income and therapeutic productivity.

Furthermore, agency executives are encouraged to use sophisticated management information systems (MIS) to replace the traditional one-on-one supervisory process. Such changes may have the added benefit of providing employees with an enhanced sense of personal mastery and commitment to the goals of the agency. Finally, agency executives and boards are encouraged to reassess their agency's physical assets, particularly real property not being used for programming. The suggestion is made that unused property should be sold and the proceeds used to further the organization's mission or to fund services to clients who lack other sources of funding.

Board Management Issues

In a managed care environment, increased pressure will also be felt by agency trustees. The relationship between CEOs and boards will change as both begin to address the issues of acceptable risk, the potential for financial loss, the need for quick decisions, and the consequences of partnership/independence decisions. Board members might do well to examine for-profit governance structures that provide CEOs with great flexibility and independence so that they might quickly respond to opportunities and crises. Boards and executives may also want to reexamine their contractual relationship to provide the latter with some protection for the career risks associated with the difficult judgements that will have to be made. Furthermore, board members' traditional role of securing private contributions will need to be reemphasized, given the importance of an endowment and an independent source of funding to the agency's mission and survival.

A Closing Thought

Child welfare agencies have traditionally emphasized client needs instead of results. To succeed in a managed care environment, agencies need to focus upon results that can be obtained by using the most cost-efficient therapeutic modalities. To proceed in any other manner is to threaten the agency's future.

References

France, A. (1883). Quoted in Safire, L., & Safire, W. (1982). *Good advice* (p. 36). New York: Time Books.

1   THE BASICS

> There is no good in arguing the inevitable. The only argument
> available with an East wind is to put on your overcoat.
> —*James Lowell [1884]*

Managed care is not a new idea. In 1929, it appeared in an early
form when teachers in Dallas, Texas, joined an organization
that, through Baylor College of Medicine, covered the costs of
hospitalization services for the group. Over time, however,
managed care has grown, taking on many forms through which
a range of health care services—going well beyond hospitalization—are financed and delivered. Importantly, managed care
now has expanded to new arenas of services, including mental
health and social services.

Managed care will continue to expand as both the private and
public health care delivery and financing sectors face rising
costs and service delivery issues. In the private sector, managed
care is becoming the predominant service delivery and financing arrangement. On the public side, growing numbers of states
are moving toward efforts to control the use of public dollars for
health care, mental health care, and social services through
managed care approaches.

At the same time, managed care has become an integral
component of the national and state focus on health care reform.
Many questions are being raised about the form that health care
financing and delivery will take in the future and the impact it
will have on providers, clients, other service delivery systems,
and the parties that pay for services.

Because managed care continues to gain ground as a financing
and service delivery strategy, child welfare service providers
must be knowledgeable about it, its terminology (see Appendix
A), and the forms it takes in the private sector as well as within

the Medicaid program. Service providers must also consider the implications of managed care for the vulnerable children, young people, and families they serve, and for the child welfare field as a whole.

What is Managed Care?

Because managed care may take a variety of forms, it defies a concise definition or description. Common to all managed care systems, however, is the integration of the financing and delivery of services. In traditional fee-for-service systems, service providers and consumers make some or most of the decisions related to the organization and delivery of services, while payers simply pay some portion of the costs incurred. By contrast, in managed care systems, payers such as insurance companies play a substantial role not only in financing services, but also in decisions related to what services will be delivered, by whom, and for how long. Three major activities characterize managed care systems: (1) arrangement for the delivery of services, (2) review of the quality and appropriateness of the services provided to those enrolled in the managed care plan, and (3) reimbursement of providers who deliver services.

Critical to an understanding of managed care is a recognition of its two major objectives—reduction of the overall costs involved in delivering services and ensuring the quality of services that are delivered.

Cost Reduction

In large part, managed care has become so pervasive because it attempts to respond to the rising costs of health care. In 1960, health care costs represented 5.3% of the Gross National Product (GNP); by 1989, health care costs accounted for 11.5% of the GNP; and by 1993, they had reached almost 14% of the GNP [Abramowitz 1993]. By the year 2000, health care costs are expected to reach $2.3 trillion or 17.3% of the GNP [Abramowitz 1993]. The spiralling cost of health care appears to be the result of a number of factors—increasingly sophisticated and expensive technology, an aging population, excess capacity of over-specialized providers, medical malpractice and/or expanding liability for medical decisions, and inflated patient demand [Abramowitz 1993; Gaucher & Coffey 1993]. Proponents of managed care point to its ability to control some of the factors driving the escalation of costs. They focus on managed care's limits on reimbursement for services and its attempts to control inappropriate use of services through mechanisms designed to review and assess access to those services, their intensity, and the length of time over which they are provided.

Risk shifting is an important cost-containment strategy used by managed care. In traditional fee-for-service arrangements, payers (usually an insurance company) bear the financial risk associated with health care coverage. Under such arrangements, if the cost of services exceeds the amount of premiums collected, the payer loses money. In many managed care systems, some or most of the financial risk in providing services is shifted from the payers to those who provide services by prepaying those providers on a set-fee basis. If the service provider's actual costs exceed the prepaid fees, the provider—not the payer—loses money.

Despite the focus on cost containment in managed care, most observers point out that, to date, risk shifting has not appreciably contained aggregate health care spending. These observations have led many to conclude that, contrary to expectations, managed care is not the solution to rising health care costs. Despite this record, however, managed care continues to be the dominant force in the health care industry, and is gaining strength in other service delivery areas as well.

Ensuring Quality of Services.

In light of managed care's focus on cost containment and reduction of unnecessary service utilization, concern is often expressed about the quality of services provided, the potential for undertreatment, and possible limitations on access to essential care. Many managed care organizations have responded to these concerns with policies and procedures that define quality, ensure that it is monitored, and direct its evaluation after services have been provided.

Most managed care systems establish or negotiate standards of care with their providers, and oversee the care that is delivered. Frequently, managed care plans incorporate standards of professional organizations, as well as those of the communities where the service providers are located.

To a growing extent, managed care plans are integrating systems that evaluate not only the process of providing services, but the outcome of services and the level of consumer satisfaction. Plans use such mechanisms as quality control (examination of the process to determine possible problems), quality assessment (identification of outliers on selected indicators, with more intensive review of the identified cases), quality assurance (feedback to low quality providers regarding deviation from good clinical practice), and quality improvement (translation of quality into administrative and work functions) [Boland 1993]. Typically, quality indicators are used to measure conformity with existing professional standards, the impact of services on the well-being of clients, the efficiency of the therapeutic setting, the intensity of service in relation to the type of client or case, and the extent to which clients are satisfied with services received [Boland 1993]. At the same time, treatment outcome (the effect of the service on client status) and treatment analysis (a determination of the cause of poor outcomes, i.e., the patient, the service provider, or the system) have become important dimensions of quality assurance and improvement.

Elements of Managed Care

Although managed care may take a variety of forms, certain elements are common to managed care arrangements as a whole:

- **Enrollment**. Individuals agree to participate in managed care plans and administratively "enroll" in a plan.

- **Single point of entry**. Individuals enrolled in managed care plans usually obtain all or most of their services through a primary care provider. This provider must approve referrals to other providers, including specialists. Unlike fee-for-service systems, in which the client/patient may obtain services from different providers without any prescreening, managed care limits choices.

- **Arrangements with selected providers to furnish a comprehensive set of services to individuals enrolled in the plan**. The group of providers selected by managed care companies is often referred to as the provider network. The goal of the managed care company is to form a network of high quality practitioners who cover a full range of primary and specialty care, and who engage in cost-effective practice. Managed care plans develop networks in a variety of ways. They may directly contract with providers, purchase other organizations with networks already in place, or rent access to an existing network.

- **Explicit standards for selection of service providers**. Increasingly, managed care companies are facing legal liability for selecting providers who render poor quality services to individuals enrolled in their plans. As a result, they are giving careful attention to selecting providers who provide quality services. Many managed care companies use specific standards to guide their selection of service providers, a process referred to as *credentialling*. These standards may be based on those developed by independent entities that set professional standards or on community practice standards.

- **Reimbursement mechanisms**. Managed care companies use a variety of payment strategies that tend to shift the financial risk to the service provider and/or control the costs of providing services. Common reimbursement mechanisms include the following:

  1. *Capitation*: a prepaid set monthly fee paid to the provider for each individual enrolled in the plan. The fee is paid in exchange for the provider's agreement to provide a range of services for individuals enrolled in the plan.

2. *Discounted UCR*: an amount that represents a reduction in the usual, customary, and reasonable (UCR) charge for the service.

3. *Fee schedules*: a listing of services with a predetermined payment for each service.

4. *Fee-for service*: payment for service as billed by the provider. Though not popular in managed care, fee-for-service has not totally disappeared, particularly as a method for paying specialists. When fee-for-service is allowed, however, it is often at a discounted rate.

A managed care company's choice of reimbursement method depends on a number of factors, including the organizational structure of the managed care plan, prevailing market characteristics, the utilization management techniques being used, and the plan's approach to risk sharing.

• **Formal programs for ongoing quality assurance and utilization review**. Managed care companies formally review quality and appropriateness of care, both to control costs and to improve quality. In some instances, they contract with utilization management firms that specialize in determining the necessity of service. Managed care companies also use gatekeeping activities (assessment and monitoring of service needs), precertification or prior approval (authorization before service is rendered), and concurrent review (assessment during service provision to monitor the need for and appropriate intensity of services). The utilization review process generally focuses on three questions:

1. Is the care medically necessary and appropriate in terms of both frequency and length of service?

2. Is effective care available at a lower cost?

3. Do patients improve because of the service?

• **Financial incentives for individuals to use plan providers and procedures**. Individuals enrolled in managed care plans

usually pay nothing or a small copayment when they receive covered services from plan providers. They generally
must pay significant out-of-pocket costs when they go to
providers who are not a part of their plan's network. In the
case of many HMOs, use of out-of-plan providers—except
in an emergency or with the approval of the HMO—is not
covered at all.

Forms of Managed Care

Managed care appears in many forms. Perhaps the most frequently encountered is the health maintenance organization
(HMO). HMOs themselves vary in form. For example, HMOs
may be *closed panel* or *open ended.* Closed-panel HMOs require
enrollees to obtain services only from the selected network
providers. Services received from providers outside the network must be paid in full by the enrollee. Increasingly, however,
HMOs are becoming open ended—allowing enrollees to receive
some reimbursement for services obtained from nonnetwork
providers. Staffing of HMOs also varies. In those HMOs referred
to as *staff HMOs,* all providers are employees of the HMO.
Network HMOs, in contrast, include providers who contract
with the HMO to provide certain services.

Other forms of managed care include organized groups of
providers under contract with a managed care organization to
provide services to individuals enrolled in plans. These groups
go by a variety of designations, including IPAs (independent
practitioner associations), PPOs (preferred provider organizations), IPOs (independent practitioner organizations), and EPOs
(exclusive provider organizations).

A major form of managed care that exists within the Medicaid
program is the prepaid health plan (PHP). PHPs resemble HMOs,
but do not provide the comprehensive range of services required
of HMOs. One type of PHP is primary care case management
(PCCM). In PCCM programs, a primary care provider renders
primary services, and at the same time, acts as a case manager,
identifying the additional service needs of the client, referring
the client to other providers, and overseeing the care provided.

Managed Care and Mental Health Care Services

As with health care costs in general, the costs of mental health care services have continued to escalate. Many believe that the costs associated with mental health care are, in fact, more difficult to control than general health care costs. They point to several factors: the subjectivity of psychological health care in contrast to the clearer indicators of physical health care; the variety of psychological care in terms of types of practitioners (psychiatrists, psychologists, clinical social workers, marriage and family counselors, and many others); the many treatment approaches and clinical orientations used to identify problems and render care; and the lack of a single standard of care for psychological services.

To a growing extent, managed care systems are covering mental health care services. Many managed care plans offer a single-service psychiatric managed care product that exists separate and apart from the general health care portion of the plan. Alternatively, many multiservice HMOs include mental health care services within their benefit package. Mental health care services offered through managed care plans vary widely, but may include outpatient mental health services, home-based services, day treatment, therapeutic family foster care, residential treatment, community-based group home services, and psychiatric hospital care. A 1992 study of 59 HMOs revealed that most HMOs provide some level of mental health care services [Fox 1992]: 98% provided outpatient mental health services, 83% provided inpatient services, and 24% offered partial hospitalization or day treatment. More than half of the HMOs provided mental health care services within the HMO itself and approximately 20% offered mental health care services through providers with contractual relationships with the HMOs [Fox 1992].

Though managed care systems may include mental health care services, they tend to limit their availability through the use of several mechanisms.

- **Conditions for receipt.** A plan may require a physician's referral prior to the delivery of services, prior authorization by the plan, or a determination that the client will be responsive to short-term treatment.

- **Coverage limits**. A plan may limit the services that can be provided in terms of a designated number of visits/days per year, an annual dollar limit, or a lifetime coverage limit.

- **Copayment requirements**. A plan may require out-of-pocket payments per visit/day or as a percentage of the total charges for services.

A number of trends appear to be developing in the provision of mental health care services under managed care. These include:

- **Payer-driven decision-making**. Managed care companies are becoming increasingly proactive and sophisticated purchasers of mental health services, and are playing an active role in the design, selection, and evaluation of mental health care products and services. Payers increasingly expect providers to have information systems in place to address the effectiveness and efficiency of the services provided. The level at which mental health care services are provided depends largely on the payers' perceptions of the cost, benefits, and value of the services.

- **Outcome orientation**. Over the last several years, it has become apparent that processes focused on quality assurance alone will no longer be sufficient for managed care companies. Instead, managed care systems have begun to use specific indicators of the actual difference that treatment makes to consumers. Companies now require that providers measure and establish clinical effectiveness in terms of improved mental health functioning.

- **Consumer sensitivity**. Increasingly, consumers are involved with payers and service providers in the area of mental health care services. They are playing a greater role in deciding what, where, and how mental health care services are provided.

Managed Care and Medicaid

In addition to changing the face of the private insurance market, managed care has come to play an increasingly important role in the Medicaid program. Three types of contractors provide most managed care services under Medicaid: federally-qualified HMOs, state-licensed HMOs, and prepaid health plans (PHPs).

Federally-qualified HMOs must meet the requirements of the Health Maintenance Organization Act of 1973 and offer specified service benefits. A federally-qualified HMO must be included upon the HMOs' request in the employee benefit plans offered by many employers. State-licensed HMOs must meet state certification requirements, which usually include a defined benefit package, quality assurance procedures, and provider guidelines.

Finally, prepaid health plans (PHPs) provide services under contract with the state Medicaid agency. Service providers receive prepaid capitated fees. PHPs, however, do not qualify as HMOs because they do not offer a sufficiently broad range of services. One prevalent form of PHP in Medicaid is primary care case management (PCCM). In PCCM programs, a primary care physician directly provides health care services and is also credentialled to manage the overall care of the patient and to coordinate access to specialized services. Physicians are paid a fee-for-service for the direct care they provide, and an additional monthly fee for case management services. Primary care physicians act as gatekeepers for any and all additional services that the patient needs.

Managed care arrangements for the delivery of Medicaid services vary in a number of ways. The plans may cover different Medicaid-eligible groups. For example, in all states that currently have managed care arrangements, AFDC-eligible individuals are included within the managed care arrangement; states vary, however, as to whether they include individuals eligible for Supplemental Security Income (SSI). States also vary in the geographical area covered by managed care (statewide or in certain communities only), in the type of managed care enrollment (voluntary or mandatory), in the type of service provider used (nonprofit, for-profit, or both), in the services excluded from their managed care contracts, and in the optional services they include under their managed care contracts.

Current Medicaid law permits five types of managed care: voluntary participation of Medicaid beneficiaries in HMOs; state inclusion of targeted case management services in the state's Medicaid plan as an optional Medicaid service; state plan exceptions that allow the development of voluntary capitated service delivery programs; freedom-of-choice waivers under which the federal government permits states to require Medicaid-eligible individuals to receive their services through a managed care capitated program (usually an HMO or PHP); and waivers under §1115(a) of the Social Security Act that allow states to use managed care approaches under Medicaid for "research and demonstration."

HMOs under Medicaid

HMOs that serve Medicaid beneficiaries are classified as either partial service providers or as comprehensive service providers. In partial capitation situations, the state contracts with the HMO to provide a narrow range of services, such as diagnostic services or dental care. Comprehensive HMO service providers must offer one of the following:

1. inpatient hospital services and one of the following mandatory services under Medicaid: outpatient hospital services; rural health clinic services; physician services; skilled nursing facility (SNF) care; early and Periodic Screening, Diagnosis and Treatment (EPSDT); family planning services; home health care services; laboratory services; or x-ray services; or

2. any three of the foregoing list of mandatory Medicaid services.

HMOs also may choose to provide, either directly or through contracts with providers, any optional service in the state's Medicaid plan, including clinic services, rehabilitative services, and inpatient psychiatric services to individuals under age 21.

Targeted Case Management Services

Within their Medicaid programs, states may choose to include targeted case management services—an optional, federally allowable Medicaid service. When designing targeted case management services, states are free to define certain populations or certain geographical areas of the state that have a particular need for case management services. Upon approval by the Health Care Financing Administration (HCFA) of the U.S. Department of Health and Human Services, states can implement targeted case management services and use them to coordinate Medicaid services received by the individuals within the defined class or geographical area.

State Plan Exceptions for Voluntary Capitated Service Delivery Programs

Though rarely used, §1915(a) of the Social Security Act allows states to design innovative managed care delivery systems, through which Medicaid beneficiaries voluntarily choose to enroll in capitated service delivery plans. Some states have explored the use of §1915(a) as a way of creating health care and social service HMOs that would provide a broad range of services to defined subgroups of Medicaid beneficiaries (such as children in state-supervised care), and would use capitation as a reimbursement mechanism. As of this writing, §1915(a) has not been used in this manner. As states turn increasingly to the use of §1115(a) (discussed below), it seems likely that §1915(a) will remain unused.

Freedom-of-Choice Waivers

Medicaid law requires, as a general rule, that beneficiaries have "freedom of choice" in their selection of service provider:

> Any individual eligible for medical assistance [under Medicaid]...may obtain such assistance from any institution, agency, community pharmacy, or person qualified to perform the service or services required (including an organization which provides such service, or arranges for their availability, on a prepayment basis).

Freedom-of-choice requires that states give Medicaid recipients the same access to services as persons with private insurance, and prevents states from "locking in" or limiting access of Medicaid beneficiaries to health care providers.

Section 1915(b) of Medicaid law allows states to implement managed care programs by waiving the freedom-of-choice requirement. If a state obtains a waiver, that is, approval from HCFA to limit consumers' choice, Medicaid beneficiaries can be required to use those providers identified by the state. Freedom-of-choice waivers have been used in several states to require certain Medicaid beneficiaries to enroll in HMOs or PHPs.

Section 1115(a) Waivers

Increasingly, states are designing Medicaid managed care programs through §1115(a) waivers. Section 1115(a) of the Social Security Act permits states, with approval from HCFA, to conduct "research and demonstration" programs that depart from federal Medicaid rules. Under §1115(a), states may operate their Medicaid programs in ways that vary from federal statutory requirements, as long as the new program is "likely to assist in promoting the objectives" of the Medicaid program, and the fiscal impact for the federal government is budget neutral. Many states view §1115(a) waivers as an opportunity to use Medicaid funds to reform their health care systems, and, in particular, contain health care costs. In addition, §1115(a) waivers give states the flexibility to establish their own Medicaid eligibility rules, service coverage, and provider arrangements. Most importantly, these waivers permit states to restrict Medicaid beneficiaries' health care delivery options by requiring them to enroll in managed care plans on a statewide basis.

Three themes are evident in the programs developed by states that have received approval for §1115(a) waivers thus far:* (1) eligibility expansion, (2) cost sharing, and (3) managed care enrollment.

Eligibility generally has been extended in all waiver states to

---

* In 1993, six states were approved for §1115(a) waivers: Oregon, Rhode Island, Tennessee, Kentucky, Hawaii, and South Carolina.

a broad group of low-income individuals, including the working poor. Upper-income limits range from 100% of the federal poverty level in Oregon to 300% in Hawaii. Several of the programs, while extending eligibility, also require cost sharing—charging individuals and families a portion of the cost of premiums, deductibles, and/or copayments, based on a sliding income scale. The use by the states of managed care arrangements* allows the delivery of a comprehensive set of Medicaid services at a per capita cost. Managed care arrangements in the §1115(a) waiver states include mandated enrollment in one of several contracted HMOs, PPOs, capitated health plans, or primary care case management programs. Figure 1 outlines the managed care features of the §1115(a) waivers approved by HCFA and commencing in 1994.

Regardless of the form it takes, the implementation of managed care under Medicaid has raised a number of questions, primarily regarding access to care and quality of services. Concerns have been expressed that the shifting of financial risk to service providers may create an incentive to underserve, and an environment in which clinical decisions may be inappropriately influenced by the cost of implementing those decisions. Equally important are concerns about reductions in the quality of care provided, particularly given the poor health status of many Medicaid beneficiaries. As §1115(a) waivers are implemented on a statewide basis, prompting widespread enrollment in managed care plans, access and quality also may become issues for special populations and individuals in rural areas that primarily had not been enrolled in managed care plans.

Implications for Child Welfare Agencies

Child welfare agency executives must meet the growing use of managed care with a solid understanding of the issues that managed care raises for the children, young people, and families

---

* All states approved for a §1115(a) waiver in 1993 have managed care features with the exception of South Carolina.

Figure 1
Managed Care Features of §1115(a) Waiver Programs

State	Program	Start Date	Managed Care Features
Tennessee	TennCare	01/01/94	All beneficiaries must enroll in one of 12 contracted HMOs or PPOs.
Oregon	Oregon Health Plan	02/01/94	All beneficiaries must enroll in one of 16 capitated health care plans or with a primary care case manager.
Rhode Island	RIte Care	04/01/94	All beneficiaries must enroll in a capitated health care plan under contract with the state.
Hawaii	Health QUEST	07/01/94	All beneficiaries must enroll in a capitated health plan under contract with the state. There are separate plans for dental services and mental health.
Kentucky	Medicaid Access & Cost Containment Demonstration Project	07/01/94	All beneficiaries must enroll in a managed care program or be assigned to a case manager.

their agencies serve, and for the agency as service provider. With regard to children in the child welfare system, and particularly those in out-of-home care, a number of questions arise as states move to implement managed care plans for Medicaid-eligible children:

- Who will choose the health care plan for the child—the parent or the state?

- Which managed care plan will be the child's plan—the parent's, the foster parent's, the state's? What plan will apply upon reunification?

- How will care be provided for children whose placements are highly transient?

- How will the child's mental health and developmental needs be met?

- Will the fact that the juvenile/family court has custody and control of children in out-of-home care have a bearing on how services are delivered through managed care?

On the one hand, managed care strategies may bring certain benefits to vulnerable children, young people, and their families, including expanded eligibility for services among the children and families that child welfare agencies serve (particularly in those states obtaining §1115(a) waivers for their Medicaid programs); increased emphasis on prevention and early intervention, with funding available to support these services; heightened accountability with clear outcome indicators and ongoing quality assurance; and added flexibility in service design and delivery, particularly where managed care arrangements involve wraparound services, home- and community-based services, and family preservation services.

On the other hand, a number of concerns must be addressed as managed care approaches are implemented, including the effects of prepaid capitated rates on service access and comprehensiveness; the extent to which the use of "medical necessity" criteria by managed care plans limits access to expensive intensive services; the design of benefit packages that fail to take into account the complex and serious needs of many of the children and young people served by the child welfare system; and geographical restrictions on enrollment and services that fail to take into account the transient placements of children in care.

As managed care becomes a reality, child welfare agencies must also consider strategic issues that will affect them as service providers. These issues include:

- How will the agency's managed care strategy align with its mission?

- To what extent can the agency's services be provided on a managed care basis? What percentage of services can—or should—be paid with managed care dollars, and what percentage with other funds?

- Which MCOs will be doing business in the agency's market, and with whom does the agency want to do business? Are there companies with whom the agency can afford not to do business? Are there companies to be avoided?

- After taking into account the full cost of the service, depreciation costs, and the risk of not being paid for services rendered, what price will allow the agency to cover its costs yet remain competitive? Child welfare agencies should consider using consultation and market surveys; carefully reviewing the costs of contract compliance, billing, and collections; and accounting for other factors such as delay in the receipt of insurance payments.

- What package of services will the agency offer to the managed care company? Does the agency want to offer intake and/or screening services, residential treatment, day treatment, therapeutic or specialized family foster care, and/or home-based services?

- Which professionals will be certified providers under the managed care program? Will the providers include social workers, psychologists, and psychiatrists?

- How will appropriate limits on the services provided be determined?

- What outcome measures will the agency use? What are the expected treatment outcomes and expected number of visits or length of stay for certain problems or diagnosis?

In addition to the above concerns, agencies will need to develop quality assurance systems that permit a review for appropriateness of services and allow for a response to problem areas. They must also carefully scrutinize the legal issues surrounding managed care contracts. Does the managed care company seek to limit the agency's ability to contract with other managed care companies in the future? What are the provisions regarding cancellation and rate increases?

As states and the private sector move increasingly toward managed care, child welfare service providers should position themselves to work effectively with managed care companies and should develop positive, ongoing relationships with the MCOs. Child welfare service providers must help managed care companies to see their agencies as important components of provider networks. MCO benefit packages need to offer the skills and expertise that child welfare agencies bring, including the ability of the agencies to work with individuals, families, and groups; their experience in delivering community-based services; their crisis intervention expertise; and their skills in developing a client-empowered environment. Child welfare agencies must encourage managed care companies to use benefit designs that include a broad continuum of care, incorporating inpatient, intermediate (i.e., day treatment), and outpatient services. Agencies can also encourage certain trends that respond to the particular needs of children and families served by child welfare agencies, such as permitting an expanded number of outpatient visits, including V-Codes (psychosocial diagnostic categories) as reimbursable diagnoses, and providing reimbursement for group care and home-based services.

Child welfare agencies should also encourage managed care companies to build into their plans such factors as quality, flexibility, client satisfaction, and case management. Effectiveness and efficiency, two managed care goals, are best served when systems are responsive to the needs of clients. Child welfare service providers are accustomed to designing and implementing such systems.

Finally, child welfare agencies should participate in the growing support for programs that promote wellness and early intervention. Increasingly, managed care organizations are emphasizing prevention and early intervention, particularly in order to limit serious health care costs in the future. Child welfare agencies can assist them in integrating such services into their benefit packages.

Participating in managed care may mean some fundamental changes for child welfare agencies. Child welfare and mental health agencies have traditionally been organized along department lines. Managed care forces organizations to integrate systems for managing the array of services — thereby requiring clinical services, administration, and plant and facility management to work together. Likewise, managed care requires that agencies view their clients as repeat customers whose satisfaction with service is paramount.

Child welfare agencies must monitor managed care developments in the private and public sectors, and, whenever possible, participate in the decision-making process regarding service design and delivery/financing approaches. Whether this process is one of working with, and marketing services to, managed care companies in the private insurance sector, or participating in Medicaid waiver decision making, child welfare agencies must be prepared and positioned to move forward.

References

Abramowitz, K.S. (1993). Changing trends in health care delivery. In P. Boland (Ed.), *Making managed health care work* (p. 25). Gaithersburg, MD: Aspen Publishers.

Boland, P. (Ed.). (1993). *Making managed health care work* (p. 10–11). Gaithersburg, MD: Aspen Publishers.

Fox, H. (1992). *Medicaid and health maintenance organizations.* Washington, DC: Fox Health Policy Consultants

Gaucher, E., & Coffey, R. (1993). *Total quality in health care* (p. 4). San Francisco: Jossey-Bass Publishers.

Lowell, J. (1883). Quoted in Safire, L., & Safire, W. (1982). *Good advice* (p. 694). New York: Time Books.

2 PREPARATION & POSITIONING

They can do all because they think they can.
                                    —*Virgil [25 B.C.E.]*

Currently, 20 states have either initiated, or have plans to initiate, managed care programs for their Medicaid population [Oss 1994]. With increasing frequency, state governments are rolling child welfare and mental health services into a behavioral health care benefit designed to serve Medicaid-eligible clients. The rush to carry out such a tremendous change in the service delivery system is being driven by three factors: (1) rising Medicaid expenditures, (2) state-by-state health care reform in the absence of federal reform, and (3) efforts to fund prevention and early intervention services. The major impetus is money—or, more accurately, the lack of it—and the impact of rising Medicaid costs on state budgets.

First, approximately half of all new state budget revenues are being used to fund the state portion of ever-increasing and unpredictable Medicaid payments. Shifting the risk of increased Medicaid payments from state budgets to insurers and service providers is the major motivation for implementing managed care. Second, the public policy debate on national health care reform, plus new flexibility from the Health Care Financing Administration (HCFA), are allowing state governors and their budget directors to experiment with Medicaid service systems. Therefore, a governor with political aspirations for a second term or for higher office has the opportunity to show how his or her state was able increase the number of people covered by health care while limiting Medicaid expenditures. By this process, the states are preempting national health care reform, and in some situations, buying themselves a five-year exemption from any future federal effort to shift costs to the states. Third, policymakers seem to carry a perception that current child welfare and mental health systems are failing to fund and provide early intervention services to prevent out-of-home care. While providers of out-of-home care and treatment view the current Title IV-E and Medicaid Rehab Option as a means to meet the needs of children with the most intensive service needs, the early intervention and family preservation position seems to dominate the public policy debate.

One can assume that the impact of managed care on the child welfare and mental health service delivery systems will be revolutionary—perhaps the greatest change in the field since the racial and religious integration of child welfare agencies in the 1960s and/or the advent of child protection laws in the 1970s. Managed care has already revolutionized the general health care delivery system and will have a similar impact on the child welfare system. Agency executives and board members need to consider how their agencies can prosper in a managed care environment, and, more importantly, how to engineer their agencies' survival during the transition.

Strategies and Tactics

Agency CEOs should concentrate on leadership and on programmatic and financial systems as they prepare their organizations for managed care, while maintaining their agencies' current level of commitment and service to children. The most dangerous period for child welfare agencies will not be once managed care is fully operational, but during the first and second year of the transition from the current system. Given the headlong pursuit of managed care by politicians and bureaucrats, mistakes and miscalculations that have a negative impact on agencies are bound to occur.

Leadership

During times of impending organizational challenge and crisis, staff and board members will be looking to their CEOs for leadership and direction. In these revolutionary times, executives of nonprofit organizations are advised to develop an entrepreneurial management style. The entrepreneurial executive is one who is "drawn to action and to fulfillment based on completion of personal and organizational milestones" [Emenhiser 1992]. The hallmark of entrepreneurial leadership is the identification of goals, a preference for action, and the tenacious pursuit of those goals.

Conversely, there is a natural human tendency to resist change, even positive change. As a species, CEOs tend to want everyone else to change, while maintaining their own prerogatives and habits. Throughout their careers, CEOs have seen the aftermath of many organizational changes and the price that organizations and individuals, especially leaders, often pay for those changes. Thus, the first step toward managed care is to prepare for change and to serve as a role model for staff and board members.

- **Preparing for leadership.** CEOs must assess themselves and their level of comfort with change. They need to learn as much as possible about managed care and behavioral health care services. Executives should begin by taking steps to serve as a change agent within their organizations and to prepare their agencies' culture for change. In short, they must prepare themselves to provide leadership.

- **Educating management.** CEOs should send management team members to managed care conferences, bring in consultants to educate staff and guide planning efforts, and use one of the managed care readiness surveys to identify weaknesses in their organizations. They will want to develop some comfort with the various learning curves of individual managers. After six months of exposure to the new reality, however, it may become apparent that some managers will not want to change or work in a managed care environment. Executives may want to keep open the option of reassigning managers who are too resistant.

- **Educating board members.** In light of the complexity of the topic and the constraints on board members' time, educating them may prove to be the greatest hurdle. Given that "no man is a prophet in his own land," CEOs should consider recruiting reputable outside consultants from professional associations to educate their board members, or using one of the managed care readiness scales already on the market;* forming ad-hoc study committees or holding special board meetings or retreats on the topic may also prove effective. Forming a board subcommittee may hold the most promise because board member-to-board member recommendations are generally more positively received than staff-to-board initiatives. As with any major decision, CEOs will want to make sure that the president and treasurer of their agencies' are prepared to support all efforts, and to serve as guides for the rest of the board.

- **Strategic planning**. CEOs should make their organizations' preparation for managed care part of their strategic plans and expand their current goals and objectives to include elements of managed care. They may also want to include elements of managed care in their organizations' vision and in their mission statements.

- **Strengthening the board**. Access to insurance company and MCO executives will become essential during the development and implementation stages of managed care marketing plans. Agencies should recruit HMO or hospital executives, or CEOs/personnel VPs from large employers who have leverage with such companies, to facilitate this access.

- **Advocacy**. Public policy involvement is crucial during the transition period. Executives should become active in advocacy efforts at all levels of government in order to participate in the design of the managed care system and insure that state and local governments do not abdicate their responsibility for severely emotionally disturbed and at-risk children. Activism at the national, state, and local levels yields the additional benefit of increased understanding of the state's managed care plan, and of how to prepare the organization for the future.

---

* These scales usually have some sections relevant to board activity.

- **Self-fulfilling prophecies**. Finally, CEOs should expect the best, but prepare for the worst. Fate has a nasty tendency of giving people what they expect, for good or ill. An optimistic approach allows people to see the opportunities that will come with the revolution of managed care. Pessimism paraded under the banner of "realism," however, invites paralysis at all levels of an organization. It is essential that CEOs help their staffs and board members to share their positive vision of their agencies' future. The greatest danger during the transition is that first the executive, then the board, and finally the staff will lose faith in their collective future and begin reacting to negative perceptions, rather than a reality that is still to be determined.

Programs

In a managed care environment, current programs will undergo a fundamental change, and, in the process, alter the ways agencies do business. Depending on the level of involvement of an agency, the principles of managed care will, for example, radically change the private agency tradition of accepting or rejecting referrals. Other program changes might include an emphasis on early intervention and prevention, utilization review, therapeutic productivity, best practice standards, and customer service. Executives should anticipate that a managed care environment will erect additional barriers to out-of-home placements and sharply reduce lengths of stay. In such settings, organizational flexibility and adaptable programming will be paramount if agencies are to efficiently meet the needs of individual children and their families. Early reports indicate that these changes may take the harshest toll on agency therapists and middle managers, who will experience great stress as they are caught between the changes initiated by upper management and the line staff's preference for continuity and maintaining the status quo.

Agency executives should consider several programmatic initiatives as they prepare for the managed care revolution.

- **Expanded continuum of care and treatment**. Agencies can prepare to offer "one-stop shopping" by providing a variety of services from intensive residential to community and family-based care and treatment and by expanding their target age range to serve children from infancy to early adulthood. Because out-of-home care will be deemphasized and lengths of stay decreased for the most expensive services, agencies should position themselves to benefit from the probable growth in outpatient services. Oss and Smith [1994] suggests that the new emphasis will be on services "without walls." Such services are relatively less intensive, are designed to meet the needs of individual clients, and demonstrate flexibility.

- **Programmatic unity and oversight**. While some agencies already offer a continuum of services, their individual programs are often quite autonomous and their staff members may resist rapid client transfer and step-downs from other departments. Agencies should reorganize, if necessary, combining admission functions, creating multidisciplinary teams, unifying clinical oversight, and preparing for ease and speed of transfer among programs. CEOs should be aware, however, that creative staff members are quite capable of appearing to accept new policies and procedures while actually acting in a manner contrary to the new reality. Unified clinical and administrative oversight, best practice standards, and a computerized client utilization tracking system will aid efforts to unify programs and monitor progress.

- **Single point of entry**. In a managed care environment, ease of admissions will be paramount, especially as agencies enter into risk-based contracts that are tied to performance and customer satisfaction. Some agencies with a broad continuum of care have multiple admission points and a confusing array of admission criteria—one agency preparing for managed care realized that it had 12 different points of entry! Agencies should unify their various admission functions to speed the acceptance process. Selecting a strong admissions director who is empowered to make speedy decisions that others must respect is vital. In a managed care environment, a 24-hour client acceptance procedure for out-of-home placement will probably be considered too slow. The compressed admissions procedures that will be necessary under managed care are a far cry from the one- to two-week process currently in place at many residential treatment centers.

- **Geographic expansion**. Agencies that have a statewide or regional base will be more attractive to managed care networks than local or center-based agencies. Agencies providing services in rural areas will have more negotiating leverage than those in urban areas where providers are plentiful. While agencies should identify and expand their service areas, they must make sure that they have the resources to provide quality services in their new outposts.

- **Outcome measures**. Although considerable debate is being waged in the behavioral health care community over which outcome measures will become the industry standard, there is no debating their necessity. Agencies that can already quantify their clients' progress will have an advantage. Those agencies that have a current research effort, or are members of the CWLA Odyssey Research Project,* should find that procedures for pre- and post-service testing, and follow-up documentation, will readily adapt to MCO demands for outcome data.

- **Customer satisfaction**. Agencies that already survey their referral sources and parents will find their efforts paying dividends when they begin to market themselves to managed care organizations. CEOs should expect, however, that the MCOs will add some items to whatever satisfaction surveys are in place. Agencies might also consider implementing focus groups to assess customer satisfaction, and

---

* For information on the CWLA Odyssey Research Project, contact Dr. Patrick Curtis, CWLA, 440 First Street, NW, Suite 310, Washington, DC 20001-2085.

recording customer feedback in a consistent manner. Those agencies who move beyond research to actual use of feedback data to improve their services and practices will have an advantage, especially under performance-based contracting.

- **Computer networks.** In a managed care organization, computer networks serve as the technological vehicle for billing, utilization review, clinical record-keeping, and tracking of client demographics. Agencies can boost office and therapeutic productivity, and greatly enhance their managements' decision-making process, by increasing their computer network capability. This may ease transitional problems that are likely to arise when government licensing and funding agencies maintain their insistence on one documentation process, while the MCOs require another, with minimal overlap. Agencies can also preserve therapist and clerical time by having data processing staff use the computer system to eliminate duplication whenever possible.

- **Therapeutic independence.** As a result of the demand for more hours of therapy, justification of service continuation, best practice standards, and the general homogenization of behavioral health care, managed care will lead to the demise of therapist and social worker independence. For example, "brief therapy" will become the new treatment modality (see Chapter 3). Agencies should expect both active and passive resistance to the new order. Some therapists might prefer private practice to organizational control and oversight. To be fair, administrators have historically encouraged lengthy stays and numerous outpatient visits because of the income such practices generate, and the difficult clinical issues faced by the children and families they serve.

- **Accessibility.** Services must be conveniently located near the plan members' homes, and office hours adjusted to meet parents' needs. Crisis intervention services will need to be available on a 24-hour basis to prevent costly out-of-home placements and provide crisis stabilization. Agencies should pay particular attention to their phone systems and the speed of staff responses to client requests.

- **Partnerships.** Accepting the concept of partnering may well be the greatest challenge for nonprofit agencies with lengthy histories and independent identities. All agencies, however, should consider joining their efforts with various types of hospitals, mental health centers, or statewide service provider networks that provide services that the agency does not (e.g., adult services, drug and alcohol, etc.) or that are in regions that expand the agency's service area. Becoming part of a large network has the advantage of generating clientele and spreading risk; the downside is that it ties the fate of the agency to that of the overall network. Agencies that decide to pursue integration with a network should look for one with similar values and establish a relationship built on trust. At some point, that trust will be tested.

- **Marketing sophistication.** Agencies should revise their marketing materials and use the language of managed care as they develop a marketing strategy to approach managed care networks. Agencies must also prepare to market themselves to those enrolled in the managed care plans. A suggested marketing strategy is outlined later in this chapter.

Finance

Because the managed care funding environment is predicated on risk and a for-profit orientation, agencies will need to radically change their funding and finance control systems. Under the current fee-for-service funding structure, agencies tend to cost-shift expenses for various programs, depending on the ability of the funding stream to support such increases. A capitation reimbursement system could largely eliminate cost shifting and would de-emphasize fee-for-service reimbursement. The key to success and survival, therefore, will be knowledge of the agency's actual cost per unit of service, and the ability to track and control service utilization and overhead expense. Deep-pocket organizations with access to an endowment or private or borrowed money will be in the best position to ride out the first years of the transition to managed care.

While some of the recommendations below may seem drastic, early reports from Tennessee and other states indicate that hasty implementation of managed care by state officials has resulted in some agencies experiencing serious cash flow problems.

- **Profit center study**. CEOs should have their accounting firms study their agencies to determine actual program costs (profit centers) and overhead expenses. In this way, they can learn the real cost per unit of each service, information that will be essential when they reach the point of negotiating contracts with MCOs. In addition, CEOs will want to solicit their accounting firms' recommendations on systems to improve their agencies' financial tracking and control systems.

- **Line of credit**. CEOs should work with their banks to substantially increase their agencies' line of credit (10% to 15% of the agency's annual budget should be adequate). If necessary, agencies should use their receivables or equipment as collateral. The agency's board of directors may be quite helpful in establishing a working relationship with a bank. Many bank officers do not grasp the workings of nonprofit organizations. Therefore, CEOs should not hesitate to "shop" the local banks for the most attractive rate and terms and to select a bank that understands the "business" of the agency, so that it can help during the transition to managed care.

- **Agency endowment**. CEOs should prepare their agencies' board members for the possibility of losses during the first years of the transition to managed care, and the possible need to dip into the corpus of endowments. While board members will have an understandable resistance to such efforts, they may be more amenable if they understand that the alternative is for them to make up any shortfall through fundraising.

- **Financial management system**. CEOs should monitor their agencies' financial situation on at least a weekly basis, and generate sophisticated finance reports and cash flow analyses for each program on a monthly basis. A management information system that combines income/expenses by program, utilization trends, and current billing will be a tremendous asset.

- **Reduction in force.** An organization's existence can quickly be placed in jeopardy if its income drops and no action is taken quickly to stem the tide of expenses. CEOs should have their management teams prepare staff reduction plans for use if funding situations turn ominous. One suggestion is to have each member of the management team develop a plan for a 20% reduction in expenses for their department. Through this exercise, team members will gain insight into what areas can be cut before hitting the muscle of operations, and how a quickly instituted hiring freeze might prevent layoffs. If nothing else, such efforts will solidify the commitment to making a successful transition. Having a plan on the shelf that was generated when there was time for careful consideration may ease its implementation and lend objectivity to a difficult situation.

- **Fundraising.** The pursuit of private donations, especially for operations, will be of great importance during the transition period. Thereafter, a steady flow of private contributions will serve as a true hedge against the vagaries of managed care, and inadvertent mistakes made during rate negotiations with the MCOs.

- **Other sources.** Federal, state, and local grants can be an important source of support and a way to distribute administrative costs. In particular, grants can provide start-up funds for new programs to expand the service continuum and for efforts to branch out into underserved areas.

Pursuing Competitive Advantage

As revolutionary changes occur in their external environments, existing organizations can either adapt to the circumstances or decline until they become societal anachronisms. With the evolution of a managed care environment, strong agencies have the opportunity to become stronger; weak agencies may disappear or be merged out of existence. Regardless of the relative strength or weakness of an agency, the greatest threat to it during the transition is if its CEO and board lose faith in its future. A pessimistic view of the future can become a self-fulfilling prophecy and derail the active pursuit of competitive advantage.

Organizational Strengths

As noted earlier, agencies that have a number of organizational strengths, or those that can position themselves in advance for managed care, will have significant advantages over their competitors. The outline below summarizes these strengths, in order of importance.

1. The organizational culture repeatedly rises to the challenge of change by expanding services, pursuing new business opportunities, and achieving goals.

2. Savvy leadership and management staff optimistically pursue new opportunities and the agency's strategic plan. Leadership is always a crucial element during a time of environmental change.

3. The board is mission oriented and cohesive, consists of people with influence or access to power, is aware of managed care, and can aid staff efforts to gain access to MCOs.

4. A system of financial monitoring and controls is in place. The agency knows the cost of its services and stands willing to reduce expenses if necessary.

5. Skilled staff members are aware of the characteristics of a managed care environment, are willing to make the necessary changes in their duties to adapt to it, and are committed to the organization's mission and vision.

6. The agency's reputation (backed up by facts and results) is one of providing quality care and treatment.

7. The agency offers a broad continuum of services, with a single point of entry and ease of admission.

8. The agency's endowment is equal to at least half of its annual budget. The board of directors is willing to access the endowment if necessary.

9. The agency has had past successes in marketing and is able to use sophisticated techniques to market itself to MCOs.

10. The agency has ongoing research efforts that generate outcome data to improve programs and assess client/funder satisfaction.

11. The agency uses a computer network for client databases, utilization review, billing, and MIS.

12. The agency holds a variety of licenses, certifications, and accreditations. Although less of an asset than in the past, these third-party "approvals" demonstrate the agency's quality. A JCAHO certification is especially helpful.

The Nonprofit Agency Advantage

In a managed care environment, three broad categories of service agencies will be competing for behavioral health care resources. Nonprofit child welfare agencies hold a number of advantages over for-profit service entities (like psychiatric hospitals) and quasi-governmental agencies (like community mental health centers). In preparation for managed care, nonprofit agencies must pursue their cost advantage over for-profit agencies, and their customer responsiveness and quality advantage over government-sponsored agencies. By aggressively marketing and promoting the benefits and differences listed below, nonprofit agencies will be able to seize the initiative during times of transition.

• **Familiarity with clientele.** Child welfare agencies have been serving children who are Medicaid eligible, abused, neglected, at-risk, and/or emotionally disabled, and their families for decades. They understand the needs of these populations, have an appreciation for their strengths, and have staffs who are skilled and culturally competent in working with them. Rumors abound that MCOs are quite confident—even arrogant—about their ability to deal with child welfare's traditional service population. One can assume that their confidence will quickly be deflated by the "dysfunctional American family" that nonprofit child welfare agencies specialize in serving. Agencies should use to the fullest the advantage of their history of service and the for-profits' inexperience.

- **Mission directed.** Commitment, caring, and concern are imbedded in the nature of nonprofit agencies—and these passions can be a potent competitive weapon. Nonprofit agencies have a sense of mission and their staffs are committed to the values of care and treatment. Such heartfelt and universal dedication adds incalculable value to the services they provide. This sense of mission is difficult to maintain in for-profit and quasi-governmental organizations, where staff members are frequently guided by either profit or regulatory mandate.

- **Competitive prices.** Perhaps the greatest advantage nonprofit agencies hold is price. In the absence of the need for a profit margin, nonprofit agencies have residential rates that are one-third those of private psychiatric hospitals, and therapy session prices that are substantially less than mental health centers and private practitioners. Many nonprofit agencies own their land and buildings. They also have organizational traditions of low administrative overhead and careful staffing patterns. While nonprofit is a misnomer (not-for-taxation would be a more accurate label), and all agencies need to have an annual surplus, nonprofit agencies are not obligated to dedicate 10% to 20% of their funds to a profit margin. Conversely, most MCOs are for-profits, and therefore will find a history of frugality appealing, even more so if the overall quality of the nonprofit agency is comparable or superior to other organizations. As for the quasi-governmental competitors, many made great strides in cost containment during the lean years of the 1980s and 1990s. For these competitors, heavy regulatory burdens, administrative percentages approaching 30%, and lack of competition in their catchment areas have generated a legacy of high rates. The nonprofit agency's mission and experience with the clientele will interest MCOs; their edge in price may well seal the bargain during negotiations.

- **Customer responsiveness.** As an extension of their mission and experience, the ability of nonprofit agencies to treat clients with dignity and respond to their needs gives them a competitive advantage over quasi-governmental entities, and, to a certain extent, over for-profits. For-profit service organizations and their staffs seem to exude a detached efficiency, which may communicate a lack of caring to the clientele. Even worse, the waiting rooms of some government-sponsored organizations may seem oppressive to the clientele. Given that the highest correlate of client satisfaction is treatment in the waiting room, all three types of service agencies would be wise to pay attention to how their organizations "feel" to their clients. Oss [1994] possibly went to the core of the issue in her question to a group of mental health providers, "Given a choice, would your clients return to your agency for service?" The ability to respond to and satisfy clients—and to quantify this ability—will be not only an initial factor in negotiations, but an essential feature of service over time.

- **Financial reserves.** Large, long-established child welfare agencies have been able to acquire operating reserves and endowments that will give them great resilience during the transition to a managed care environment. These resources provide an edge for them over the quasi-governmental agencies that have generally used the government as their source of reserve. Independence and financial resources may offer nonprofit agencies some protection during the "merger mania" that will result in the elimination of many government-sponsored service providers. Financial strength can be a strong selling point in marketing an agency to an MCO.

- **Housing**. Therapeutic services, combined with residential, foster family, and group care housing, will be a substantial niche market in behavioral health care service provision. While MCOs may try to limit the use of out-of-home care, their prior successes in reducing psychiatric hospitalization lengths of stay will probably not be replicated with child welfare services. Unlike private pay clients, child welfare agencies serve children who generally have nowhere else to go and few of them have supportive family waiting in the wings at the end of their stay. When the competitive price advantage is combined with the continuum of housing and the care options nonprofit child welfare agencies offer, a substantial advantage over for-profit and quasi-governmental organizations is formed. Nonprofit agencies seeking to combat the potential decrease in their residential occupancy might look toward improving their diagnostic capability and crisis stabilization services. They might also present their residential program as a low-cost alternative to both freestanding and general hospital-based psychiatric placements. In addition, group care and family foster care networks can be marketed as relatively less expensive "step-down" options for children who are not likely to return home in the near future.

- **Community visibility**. One of the great benefits of a managed care system is its promotion of early intervention and prevention. Therefore, MCO contracts with child welfare agencies will probably contain stipulations regarding outreach, accessibility, and marketing of services to plan members. Agencies can use their history and their resulting community visibility to promote themselves to the MCOs. While the government-sponsored agencies may have similar recognition in the community, child welfare service providers will have an edge over newly incorporated public and private service providers. Many local marketing and opinion research firms conduct household surveys. They are usually willing to add a question or two about nonprofit agencies at little or no cost. Agencies should use such services to quantify their visibility, then use that information in their managed care marketing efforts.

Marketing to Managed Care Organizations

All of an agency's strategic planning and preparation efforts will be for nothing if it is unable to market its services to the MCOs. In an operational sense, the success or failure of an agency's efforts will largely be determined by its ability to identify, access, and sell itself to the MCOs that stand astride the referral and resources allocation process. Agencies should focus on both the basics of organizational marketing, and specific recommendations on the process of selling to this new market segment.

The standard business school definition of marketing identifies it as "the anticipation, management, and satisfaction of demand through the exchange process" [Evans & Berman 1984]· A real-world definition would be "the optimistic pursuit of opportunity, through the interaction of faith and fate." Certainly, psychological research has caught up with the common sense notion that an optimistic approach to life is a powerful determinant of everything from professional success to physical longevity [Seligman 1990]. Opportunity abounds in the emerging field of managed care. And it is precisely the revolutionary aspects of managed care that create an environment where faith and optimism can so powerfully determine the future of individuals and institutions. The very volatility of the situation provides agencies with an opportunity to be in the right place at the right time.

Another way to describe aspects of both faith and optimism is self-motivation. In a recent book on the nature of entrepreneurs, editors Ray and Renesch [1994] present the argument that one's motivation is the result of the difference between one's current circumstances and one's expectations. Therefore, people are

quite motivated when their minds perceive a great distance
between the two, and correspondingly, their motivation actually decreases as they draw near their expectation and shift to a
maintenance mode. Those familiar with social psychology will
recognize this description as an updated version of Festinger's
[1957] groundbreaking work on cognitive dissonance. Whether
the concept is accepted psychology or an entrepreneurial article
of faith, the secret is to constantly raise expectations to generate
the required motivation. The advice to the head of an organization embarking upon marketing efforts in the realm of managed
care is the same—become uncomfortable with the current state
of affairs and set high expectations for the agency and the
marketing effort.

Developing an agency's marketing plan consists of identifying
goals, selecting prospects, gaining access to the prospects, and
selling the agency's strengths. Selling simply consists of taking
the needs of the MCOs and matching them with the agency's
services, then using the personal relationships that develop
during this interaction as the vehicle for achieving a sale. For
some human service professionals, however, the thought of
needing to sell themselves and their agency sounds too profit
oriented. In such instances, the marketing plan should be viewed
as a process of expanding the agency's network to serve additional clientele.

Goals

The CEO's first order of business is to set high expectations
regarding the success of the agency's marketing efforts. These
expectations need to be optimistic enough to stretch the abilities
of staff members, and to be worthy of their additional efforts.
The number of marketing visits (sales calls) and the time frames
need to be established and matched to a reporting and monitoring process. This process should have great visibility within the
agency's management team and organization. High standards
again require the intervention of leadership that is confident of
the agency's future, and able to convince (sell) the staff on their
importance.

CEOs will want the goal setting process to be a mutual effort between the leader and the agency's promotion staff. They should outline their organizational needs, then let the staff determine objectives and time frames. The number of marketing visits may actually be higher and the time frames shorter than those of the CEO; certainly, the staff's motivation to achieve these goals will be worth the effort to involve them.

Recruiting staff members who are capable of responding to the challenge is crucial. People in the agency who have demonstrated leadership, convinced families of their abilities, or shown success in selling themselves to groups during training sessions, are possible candidates.

Lastly, one of the axioms of good salesmanship is belief in the product being sold. A passionate belief in the organization and its good works will be one of the most important elements of the search for the right person/people.

Geographic Market

Another important aspect of the agency's marketing plan is the geographic territory the agency plans to serve. As noted above, agencies that provide services regionally or statewide will have an advantage over local organizations. In selecting the target market area, CEOs need to make decisions that generate a balance between geographic expansion and insuring that their organizations are capable of providing quality services throughout the target area. The latter is particularly important, given the emphasis in managed care on accessibility, quality, and visibility. For those CEOs contemplating geographic expansion, priority should given to areas from which their agencies already receive referrals (especially for out-of-home care services), underserved areas (usually rural), and urban areas where the agency can bring to the market a unique and attractive service not currently provided. Once an agency has made the decision to expand (and balanced its service expansion against possible overextension), staff can begin the process of prospect identification.

CEOs should expect a competitive response to their agencies

geographic expansion. Movement into new territory may result in some controversy among collegial agencies, probably as a result of two factors: (1) the perceived violation of the traditional roles of nonprofit agencies, and (2) fear.

Traditionally, private and public funders have encouraged nonprofit agencies to cooperate rather than compete. The creation of a managed care environment, however, encourages competition among agencies. Of course, some have always been at odds with the traditional cooperation mentality, preferring instead to view "friendly competition" among agencies as a plus for clients, and as a means of improving all services in a community, the underlying assumption being that there is plenty of work to go around, and that clients and funders will be attracted to the best quality services. The transition period into a managed care environment will initially move the cooperation vs. competition debate in the direction of greater competition; after this transition period, however, it will probably result in greater integration among agencies.

Fear will be a more difficult obstacle to overcome than the competition hurdle. As agencies become fearful about their future, the entry of another agency into their "market" will be viewed with suspicion and possible hostility. Unfortunately, some agency executives will concentrate on what they have to lose, instead of pursuing the new opportunities presented by managed care. Regrettably, fear and increased competition will generate some conflict during any agency's geographic expansion. CEOs should anticipate it, but not let it set the boundaries of their agencies' service territory.

Prospect Identification

The prospect identification process will focus on a small group of MCOs that are operating in the agency's target territory. In the world of marketing, this would be referred to as a market segmentation plan. A segmentation strategy focuses on determining the needs, characteristics, and similarities of a small, relatively homogeneous group of customers. By developing research profiles on the MCOs' needs, agencies can custom design their sales strategy to increase their chances of success.

For those in the nonprofit world, prospect identification is analogous to conducting a feasibility study before embarking on a capital campaign. One principle in fundraising is that prospect research is crucial to the success of the campaign. Capital campaign procedures—identifying potential donors, gaining access, interviewing about philanthropic priorities, and constructing a profile on each prospect for future reference—can be adapted to the market research phase of the managed care marketing effort.

As for the finer points of prospect identification, agencies should use both their government sources and their trustees to determine which MCOs are operating in their area. For agencies in states where managed care initiatives are being driven by the state government, a number of resources are available.

Once the governor's office or state budget agency announces the intent to move toward managed care, the major national MCOs will begin seeking state insurance commission approval to operate. In states with large populations, such an announcement can trigger the equivalent of the Oklahoma land rush, as companies seek to gain a foothold. Because most of the insurance commissions operate under various state versions of open records laws, agencies can gain access to the MCOs' applications (or a summary), which will generally list the officers, addresses, number of current covered lives, financial information, and an enormous amount of other valuable information about the company.

Furthermore, state agencies responsible for implementing managed care can provide a wealth of information about the form it will take and the most likely players. CEOs should use their contacts with state officials and employees to gain an inside track on prospect identification. Occasionally, contacting a state agency official who is dissatisfied or concerned about the turn of events may provide insight into the process that is not available from other sources.

Finally, most state governments are also part of the Internet system, or are tied electronically to library and university systems, allowing users to access relevant information about managed care via their computer networks.

Access

Most states moving toward managed care will be issuing request for proposals (RFPs), especially for basic health care plans to cover traditional Medicaid clients. These RFPs can provide a wealth of information about state intentions, demographics, and demands in regard to prospective MCO organizational structures and approaches to service provision. Agencies should use their state contacts to either get on the mailing list for or otherwise obtain a copy of the RFPs.

After the MCOs submit their proposals, the state will make its selection of those MCOs that will serve the various regions of the state. Agencies should obtain a copy of this information to find out which MCOs will be operating in their service territory. This list will become the most important document for guiding the agency's marketing and prospect identification efforts. With a list of prospects in hand, agencies can obtain the targeted MCOs' managed care proposals by using their states' open records and bidding integrity laws to their advantage. In effect, agencies can use the MCOs' own proposals to do much of their segmentation research for them, learning how the MCOs plan to provide service, how their leadership and organization are structured, what services will be provided and where, etc. In short, these applications provide a marketing encyclopedia of service needs, and provide guidance as to how an agency can begin to fulfill those needs at a reasonable price.

One complementary approach to the above is for CEOs to use their agencies board of directors and community contacts to initiate the marketing process [Emenhiser 1992]. Many of the agencies featured in Chapter 4 initiated their entry into managed care on the strength of their board of directors' involvement with the health care and insurance industries. Agencies might consider organizing ad-hoc committees comprising their board members and knowledgeable members of their communities to guide their managed care preparation and marketing efforts. Such committees can identify and access those who head managed care firms. With such access, CEOs can apply the feasibility study strategy of interviewing the managed care prospect about its future needs and desires, thereby enlisting the prospect's assistance in designing the marketing plan. These "cultivation calls" also help to establish the agency's credentials and launch a relationship with the MCO executives.

Another approach to gaining access to MCOs is a straightforward letter requesting the opportunity to meet with the CEO or a representative (see Appendix B for a sample). In their letters, CEOs should outline their intent and the topics of interest. The letter can also serve as an opportunity to outline the strengths of the organization. The letter should ask the recipient to alert his or her executive secretary to expect a call from the agency CEO, thereby avoiding the usual barriers that executives construct to protect their time.

The end result of any of these plans is to gain access to the highest level personnel in the MCO. It is amazing what people are willing to do for an agency once they are approached officially.

Public Relations and Marketing Firms

Agencies may want to consider the costs and benefits of using a professional public relations (PR) firm to develop their marketing plans. PR and marketing firms that specialize in market segmentation campaigns can work with agencies to identify prospects, analyze particular needs, and outline the best means to promote the agency as the answer to those needs. Using a PR firm that has hospital, insurance, or other health care clients is a plus, as agencies may be able to use the PR firm's contacts to gain access.

A PR firm can develop marketing materials that communicate the quality of the organization, and, with the guidance of the CEO, use the language of managed care. If the agency can obtain copies of the annual reports and the marketing materials of the targeted MCOs, it can use the PR firm's graphic design staff to match the style and quality of the targeted MCOs' publications.

Involving a PR firm in the marketing effort is especially beneficial in situations where there is little time, the agency's marketing materials need a substantial upgrade, or the CEO feels that the use of an outside consultant will help the management team focus on the importance of the transition.

Closing the Deal

The last step in the marketing plan is the personal selling phase, in which CEOs use personal relationships, knowledge of their prospects' needs, and their agencies' strengths to gain a sale. As noted above, the key element is the ability of CEOs and their agency staff to sell themselves and their agencies, while building a personal relationship with prospects. Even though many human service professionals are quite adept at selling themselves to their colleagues and clients, they often have difficulty with this concept of salesmanship. CEOs who have solid, confident staff members who are sold on the agency's services can overcome this difficulty by having those staff members join in on the first few marketing calls. Over time, staff members will become enamored with the managed care possibilities and their instrumental role in propelling the agency into a more secure future.

Summary

The ever expanding role of managed care in the child welfare and mental health fields will change—perhaps radically—the way agencies are funded and how they deliver services. While there is concern about how managed care systems will be implemented, there are steps CEOs, agency board members, and staff members can take to prepare for the transition and prosper during the aftermath. The greatest danger during the transition is of the executives and board leadership losing faith in the future of their agencies and in the need of children for quality care and treatment.

References

Emenhiser, D. (1992). *Power funding: Gaining access to power, influence and money in your community* (p. 123, 141–142). Rockville, MD: The Taft Group.

Evans, J. R., & Berman, B. (1984). *Essentials of marketing* (p. 7). New York: MacMillan Publishing Company.

Festinger, L. (1957). *A theory of cognitive dissonance* (p. 117). Stanford, CA: Stanford University Press.

Oss, M. [1994, August]. Speech made before Montgomery County, OH, mental health care providers.

Oss, M., & Smith, A. (1994). *Behavioral health practice management audit workbook* (p. 4). Gettysburg, PA: Behavioral Health Industry News, Inc.

Ray, M., & Renesh, J. (Eds.) (1994). *The new entrepreneurs: Business visionaries for the 21st century* (p. 86). New York: Sterling & Stone, Inc.

Seligman, M. (1990). *Learned optimism: The skill to conquer life's obstacles, large and small* (p. 16). New York: Random House.

Virgil (25 B.C.E.]. Quoted in Safire, L., & Safire, W. (1982). Good advice (p. 262). New York: Time Books.

3   IMPLEMENTATION

If you think you can win, you can win. Faith is necessary to
victory.
                                                    —William Hazlitt [1819]

Capitation payment models in health care financing have been
in existence in the United States for more than a decade. They
were developed to enable insurance companies and employers
to predict their health care costs for an entire year. Capitation
means that an insurance company (or large employer with a self-
insurance plan) pays an intermediary company such as a managed care organization (MCO) or a service provider a set fee per
member to deliver some or all of the services provided under a
health care plan. Behavioral health care benefits are commonly
provided separate from medical or surgical benefits, an arrangement referred to as a carve-out.

With behavioral health care carve-outs, the payer (an insurance company, MCO, or employer) pays an agreed-upon fee
(ranging from $1.50-$5.00) per member per month, in return for
which the provider agrees to provide all contracted for services.
Although there are almost as many payment and plan variations
as there are plans, payment rates are normally based on several
factors: (1) the basic plan benefit, (2) whether or not the service
provider can collect any copayments, (3) utilization history of
the plan members (if this information is available), and (4) the
number of enrollees in the plan. Generally, the more enrollees
a plan has, the lower the payment per enrollee.

The decision to enter into a capitation contract means entering into uncertainty at a level greater than that generally experienced by most agencies. The job of all administrators, however, is to manage the reality of uncertainty to the greatest extent
possible. Uncertainty can be reduced to some extent when

service utilization is managed and appropriate alternatives to inpatient treatment are available.

Some variables are beyond the control of service providers. For example, behavioral health care service providers cannot control a sudden increase in service use because of a rash of adolescent suicides in their community, which may create an environment in which many youths or their parents seek mental health services for situational crises or precautionary reasons.

Predictability of Capitation Contracts

The definition of reasonable reimbursement largely depends on whose perspective it is viewed from—that of the MCO or that of the service provider. MCOs often view reasonable reimbursement as a rate that is lower than that paid by competitors, and that remains predictable. Service providers generally view reasonable reimbursement as a rate that allows them to provide quality services at a break-even cost or for a slight profit.

There are trade-offs between predictability of costs and rates. Discounted fee-for-service reimbursement contracts, where set payments are made to service providers as services are used, provide low cost, but with some risk. Although usage predictions are made in such arrangements, the MCO assumes the risk that use may exceed the predicted rates. MCOs may gain predictability in total annual costs, however, by choosing to pay a capitation rate higher than their expected fee-for-service rate.

An example of this positive trade-off for MCOs and service providers is a situation in which the expected cost per member per month (under a negotiated fee-for-service contract) is $4.50 for mental health services. Actual utilization, however, could bring the cost to $6.00 per member per month. A number of factors could contribute to the increased utilization and increased cost, such as inadequate gate keeping or a public event such as an earthquake. The MCO may be willing to pay a capitation rate of $5.25 per member per month to achieve predictability in costs. Under this scenario, a well-managed service provider may be able to receive more revenue under a capitation contract than it would under a discounted fee-for-service contract.

Shared Risk/Shared Gain

For capitation payment models to benefit all parties (payers, service providers, and service consumers/clients), a number of systems have to be in place. The service provider needs: (1) adequate information concerning its cost, (2) a utilization management system in place to control and monitor usage in order to confine it to the expected norms, and (3) historical utilization information concerning the population of insured lives to be served.

Quality and Cost Control

Service providers must have quality primary care physicians in their service delivery systems. They must also have well-organized intake and triage systems that prescreen clients for medical problems and inappropriate requests for behavioral health care services. Many capitation contracts include quality and cost control rewards. If utilization of inpatient days of care remains below certain agreed-upon targets, but quality remains at expected levels, service providers may receive bonus payments or share in MCO profits. Although low inpatient utilization would not appear to matter to the payer at first glance, it does make a difference over time. If service providers have higher than expected inpatient utilization over an extended period of time (such as two years), eventually they will need higher capitation payments or they will go out of business, forcing the MCOs to select another provider, which in turn disrupts the continuity of care. Assuming service quality was high, such changes are a negative from an insurance company marketing perspective. Rewards and penalties for the primary care physicians can facilitate prescreening.

The capitation model may have several variations in which service providers might participate. In a subcapitation model, organization A may be fully capitated at $5.00 per member per month for mental health services. In turn, it may enter into a subcapitated contract with organization B for B to provide outpatient, partial hospitalization, and residential treatment services. Organization A would make a set capitation payment to organization B for these specific services, based on the projected cost per service unit and expected utilization rates.

Setting the Capitation Rate

Historical utilization data is essential in determining whether capitation rates are realistic. Table 1 provides an example of how service providers can arrive at a capitation rate by projecting their costs and service utilization, based on the major services required by most managed care companies. Some MCOs allow inpatient days to be used at a ratio of two residential days to one hospital day.

Agencies that operate residential treatment and/or treatment family foster care home programs as alternatives to hospitalization, would, in all probability, decrease costs substantially and could serve the hypothetical population with a lower capitated rate, as shown in table 2. The cost projection in table 2 assumes a low usage rate and is based on hypothetical usage information for the prior two to three years that should be provided by the MCO with which the service provider is contracting. To determine the actual per member per month reimbursement rate, service providers need to determine the cost of risk and their desired profit margin, keeping in mind that, while utilization rates may increase at any time, in most situations capitation rates will only be increased once a year. In negotiating a capitation rate, service providers should build in a profit margin of 5% to 10%, and an utilization increase risk factor of 15% over the previous highest level.

Table 3 provides an example of actual utilization results by service modality for a capitated plan serving 62,150 children and adolescents. The numbers are rounded for clarity.

Determining the Level of Risk

Capitation contracts have generally been determined to be too risky if the total population to be served is less than 25,000. If the

Table 1
Calculating a Capitation Rate—Major Services*

[Sample Population—26,000 Children and Adolescents]

	# Users per 1000	# of Service Units per User	# of Annual Service Units	Cost per Unit	Total Annual Cost
Inpatient	5	20	2,600	$500	$1,300,000
Partial Hospital.	2	25	1,300	$237	$308,100
Outpatient	30	20	15,600	$95	$1,482,000

Total Annual Cost—$3,090,100
Cost Per Member Annually ($3,090,100 divided by 26,000)— $118.85
Cost Per Member Per Month ($118.85 divided by 12)—$9.91
* All numbers are for purposes of example only.

population to be served is that small, service providers may want to develop a shared risk contract, in which additional compensation would be provided if the incident rate of hospitalization or residential treatment exceeds normal rates and that unpredicted usage is based on high acuity levels, rather than poor utilization management by the service provider.

The capitation payment rate should be relatively higher when the number of enrollees is low. As the size of the population to be served approaches 50,000, service providers should be able to spread the risk effectively and have a reduced number of peaks and valleys in requests for services.

Services

Insurance companies have historical data bases reflecting the average cost per member (by age group and ethnicity) in each region in which they do business. When capitation rates are set, this information is taken into account. Capitation rates are also based on the assumption that most people should receive their behavioral health care services on an outpatient basis, using a problem-focused, therapeutic model. Therefore, service providers considering capitated contracts should have a well-developed array of outpatient programs at sites convenient to the

Table 2
Calculating a Capitation Rate—Residential Treatment*

[Sample Population—100,000 Children and Adolescents]

	# Users per 1000	# of Service Units per User	# of Annual Service Units	Cost per Unit	Total Annual Cost
Residential Treatment	2	26	5,200	$275	$1,430,000

Total Annual Cost—$1,430,000
Cost Per Member Annually ($1,430,00 divided by 100,000)— $14.30
Cost Per Member Per Month ($14.30 divided by 12)—$1.19
* All numbers are for purposes of example only.

plan's clients. Service providers who lack outpatient and crisis response services (and who choose not to provide these services) should form partnerships with organizations that do and that are willing to participate in the contract's risk and reward sharing.

Probably the most important service or function in a capitation environment is an initial intake triage service. This service should be backed up with a 24-hour on-call staff availability and immediate access to service. An excessive number of hospital admissions can destroy the financial viability of a capitation contract. Such admissions often occur not out of clinical necessity, but because a crisis arises after hours or on weekends, when adequate triage and crisis intervention systems are not in place. A system of crisis response is needed that engages the family in the appropriate service. While this may include brief hospitalization, typically, relatively less restrictive and less costly services will be necessary.

Those child welfare agencies entering into capitated payment contracts that do not operate psychiatric hospitals—and most do not—must affiliate or contract with organizations that operate such facilities and that share a compatible treatment philosophy. Where the child welfare agency is receiving the capitation payment, the hospital may provide its services on a fee-for-service basis. The most common model is for one or more

Table 3
Sample Capitation Insurance Plan*

[62,150 Children under Age 18 Enrolled in Plan]

	# Users per 1000	# of Service Units per User	# of Annual Service Units	80% of Std. Fee	Total Annual Cost	Cost per Member Annual	Cost per Member Monthly
Outpatient	10	11	6,837	$76	$519,574	$8.38	$0.70
Hospital	4	6	1,492	$480	$715,968	$11.52	$0.96
Partial Hospital.	2	15	1,865	$260	$484,770	$7.80	$0.65
Intensive Residential	.5	25	777	$320	$248,600	$4.00	$0.33
					========	======	=====
Total Fee for Service					$1,968,912	$31.70	$2.64

* All numbers are for purposes of example only.

psychiatrists, primarily associated with the child welfare agency, to be responsible for hospitalizing children and managing the treatment during the period of hospitalization. This goes far toward ensuring continuity of treatment and treatment philosophy.

The Service Array

To develop systems of care that have an opportunity of succeeding under capitated contracts, service providers must expand their existing services and add new ones. Most agencies have implemented systems that offer a broad array of services, generally including some combination of those shown in figure 2.

The development of relatively less restrictive services has the potential to enhance the quality of the services provided, and increases the probability that services can be provided at a profit under capitated payment plans. Clearly, the service delivery system must have incentives, both financial and clinical, to keep hospital and residential treatment usage to a minimum.

Coordination of Adult Services with Children's Services

Some MCOs require their service contractors to manage or directly provide adult and child/adolescent services. Generally,

---

Figure 2
The Service Array

Nonresidential Services	Residential Services
Assessment	Therapeutic foster care
Psychiatric services	Therapeutic group care
Outpatient services	Crisis residential services
(individual, family, and group)	Residential treatment
Home-based services	services
Day treatment	Inpatient hospital services
Crisis services	
After-school and evening programs	
Therapeutic respite services	
Behavioral aide services	
Case management	
Parent education and support services	

---

agencies are better off focusing on child and adolescent services, if that is their specialty, and to have the MCO purchase adult services directly from another provider. If the MCO chooses to deliver its behavioral health care services through a single capitated contract, child-serving agencies might look into partnering with organizations that provide adult services, and jointly seeking the capitated contract. In such a scenario, one of the organizations would actually hold the contract and subcontract to the other. The organization holding and managing the contract would receive compensation for managing the contract, and for having the lead role in assuring contract compliance and managing the risk associated with higher than planned utilization, as well as any legal risk associated with the contract.

Contract and Rate Negotiations

In all negotiations, understanding the probable negotiating positions of the other party is an important factor. In addition to seeking capitated contracts at reasonable cost, MCOs are also interested in establishing long-term contractual relationships, selecting providers with good reputations, and selecting providers with sufficient resources to accept some financial risk.

Frequent changes in service providers are detrimental to MCOs in terms of the cost of having to once again prepare and issue requests for proposals, enter into contract negotiations, and reprise their start-up efforts. Clients often complain if they have to change providers, especially those clients with chronic problems. Selecting service providers with good reputations is essential for successful MCO marketing, and for long-term risk management purposes.

Service providers' proposals should address each of these concerns. Generally, written proposals should be submitted at the first negotiation session. These initial proposals will frequently become the framework for future negotiations and can set the tone for the negotiating sessions.

Acquiring cost and historical utilization data, as set forth earlier in this chapter, enables service providers to accurately analyze the expected costs to be incurred in serving the target population. If analysis shows dramatic changes in usage from year to year, it may be a sign that future usage may be too unpredictable—and the opportunity for loss too great under a capitated contract.

Before beginning negotiations, MCOs will determine the minimum and maximum capitation rates they will consider. Interested service providers will need to conduct research on the prevailing capitation rates for behavioral health care services in their regional market.

Service providers must sell quality, however, and not just the lowest cost. Nonprofit agencies should not assume that they are the lowest-cost provider in the market. Some for-profit organizations with extensive outpatient capability can deliver services at a lower cost because they lack accreditation and often pay their clinicians on a contract basis without benefits. In addition, for-profit multisite residential treatment providers may have lower costs than nonprofit residential treatment programs due to a number of factors, including mass purchasing capabilities and shared human resources management.

Service providers should consider presenting their initial bid with a capitation rate that is in the 75th percentile in the market, and state their capability for delivering quality services. Capitation rates for behavioral health care services for children and adolescents (including outpatient and inpatient services) generally range between $1.50 and $5.00 per member per month. In some markets, competitive insurance pricing may keep the rates so low that it may not be possible to deliver a quality service. Consequently, it may not be in the service provider's best interest to participate in capitated contracts in such a market.

If a child welfare or children's mental health care agency becomes the contractor in a capitated payment service delivery contract, it must have the capacity to accept and manage the risk, both in terms of potential financial loss and in terms of adequate insurance coverage for potential legal liabilities. Many insurance companies require certain financial reserves and will review agency audits and recent financial statements. The reserve requirements will generally correlate with the risk being assumed by the service provider and the insurance company. Generally, agencies should have reserves equal to three months projected reimbursement from the company; those reserves should be dedicated to backing performance of the specific capitated contract. For example, if there are 30,000 enrollees in the plan, and the capitation rate is $2.30 per member per month, the monthly payment to the service provider would be $69,000. In this example, the reserves should be approximately $207,000. Some agencies may be able to arrange for a line of credit to serve as the reserve requirement, assuming such arrangements are satisfactory to the insurance company.

Changing the Organizational Culture

Historically, most child welfare agencies have served large numbers of public agency clients and low-income families and their children. While agency leaders are sensitive to the needs of these traditional client populations, they may lack experience in meeting the needs of insurance company staff, parents who are skilled in advocating for their needs, and employers who are actually paying for services rendered. To succeed under

capitated managed care, agencies must change. These changes
need to permeate the entire organization.

Clinical staff need to respond to parents, children, insurance
company representatives and employer representatives in a
timely, professional manner. Their relationships are likely to be
more like partnerships than the typical clinician-client relationship. Flexibility in the scheduling of appointments (including
providing weekend and evening hours), and candor in sharing
treatment information are examples of practices more common
in private managed care service delivery than in public agency
contracted services.

As necessary, written informed consents must be obtained
from parents to permit the appropriate exchanges of information
to facilitate this partnership. In some situations, parents may
feel pressured to allow their employers to have clinical information. Service providers need to recognize these situations and to
help facilitate appropriate exchanges of information that do not
compromise their clients' right to reasonable privacy.

The service provider's business offices need to be efficient
and responsive to clients. Parents in private insurance plans
who receive their services from child welfare agencies will
compare the service provider's business offices with those of
hospitals and physicians. Fee-setting and collection procedures
should be of high quality, and should convey an organizational
climate that reflects concern and compassion, combined with a
strong sense of business acumen.

The physical plant should be maintained at a quality level that
is competitive with for-profit clinics and behavioral health care
hospitals. Repairs should be promptly completed. Inpatient
units should be so designed and maintained as to convey the
high value placed on the children served and the needs of all
family members. Parking availability, outdoor safety and lighting, and distance from the parking area to the entrance of the
building should be reviewed and modified as needed to make
facilities client friendly.

In capitated contracts of long duration, some families may
access services several times over the life of the contract. This is
especially true in situations in which the child's condition is

chronic. Staff members must be trained to view clients as potential repeat customers and to provide services that are so appealing that the clients would return even if their managed care contracts did not require them to do so.

Generally, MCOs survey their insured members and their employers to determine their level of satisfaction on a number of indicators, and report their findings to the service providers. Those service providers who would prefer to receive a good report card and not wait to be told what needs to be changed should conduct their own customer surveys each quarter and make changes accordingly. The results should be shared with all agency staff, as the entire organization must work together to facilitate change successfully. Consideration should be given to annually sharing a summary of these survey results with those MCOs with whom the service provider has contracts. More importantly, service providers should communicate changes they have made in response to the survey results.

Brief Treatment Focus

The expression "the meter is running" clearly applies to capitated contracts. Clinical staff must learn to focus on helping children and their families identify the most urgent problems. Timelines have to be agreed to, and parents need to be informed at intake as to what is expected from them. Capitated contracts assume brief, problem-focused interventions. Service providers should not enter into capitated contracts without adopting a brief therapy and least restrictive treatment philosophy.

Clinical staff in most nonprofit child welfare and mental health care organizations have to accept thorough training. They must also accept the reality that in some cases where there is need, services will have to be denied if the insurance contract does not provide adequate coverage. Staff will have to understand that services frequently must be discontinued earlier than most clinicians think best, even though the family could benefit from additional services. Provider organizations may choose to provide those services to the client on a fee-for-service basis, including a sliding fee scale—if funds are available to subsidize the care and treatment.

It is important to remember that capitation contracts are almost always associated with HMO plans, and employees often have an option of selecting a plan other than the HMO. Thus, by paying higher premiums, clients may have increased benefits for behavioral health care services. Consequently, the employees' HMO coverage must assume some responsibility for limited benefits. If employees chose the "low cost" insurance option, it should not become the responsibility of the service provider to provide services not intended in the "cap" contract. Clinicians must be given the necessary administrative support to work effectively under capitated payment contracts. When providing capitated services, utilization management staff must frequently communicate with clinical staff about utilization norms (expected number of days of inpatient services or number of counseling sessions), and what the projected utilization is for each clinician and each program. The utilization management staff should take the lead in helping clinicians identify alternative treatment options for difficult cases. It is these cases that often have a negative impact on the financial viability of capitated contracts by requiring services and costs in excess of expected norms.

Provider organizations designed around work teams are more functional and successful than highly structured, hierarchical organizations in which key staff, such as the quality improvement manager or the utilization manager, are not given the direct opportunity to communicate with clinicians, impact the quality of care, or affect the length of services. Open communication enables creative solutions involving the clients. One example is an organization that utilizes an emergency shelter, combined with intense therapy, as an alternative to hospitalization; in such cases children are not considered dangerous to themselves or others, but treatment for a brief period of time cannot be successfully provided on an outpatient basis.

Outcome Measurements

The child welfare and mental health care fields must improve their evaluation and outcome research to address global questions. Studies that determine results of placement in various settings, ranging from shelters to psychiatric hospitals, must occur with increased frequency, and the results should be better publicized than is currently the case.

In addition, service providers contracting with MCOs under capitated contracts and/or managed care contracts should, at a minimum, measure the following: (1) recidivism rates, (2) results of treatment (using instruments that measure client behavior and mental status at admission and discharge), (3) treatment results compared against diagnosis and type of service provided, and (4) percentage of clients discontinuing services against clinical advice.

The results of such measurements should be used to make changes in how services are provided. In addition, outcome data should be shared with the MCOs. In long-term partnerships with MCOs, such data can form a basis for changes in benefits, capitation rate, and the array of services offered by the service provider organization. Most importantly, the data communicates to the service provider's staff and to the MCO the agency's commitment to quality services and its willingness to understand its own weaknesses so that changes can be made.

Conclusion

Paul H. Keckley, Ph.D., chairman of the Keckley Group, a health care consulting corporation, posits that service providers are functioning in an environment in which the payers distrust most providers. The payers are suspicious of profiteering in mental health—especially in light of the activities of several major psychiatric hospital chains that have demonstrated a propensity for "strip mining" in attracting patients with appropriate insurance. Lacking definitive outcome data, payers have to make their decisions based on costs, which have increased substantially in recent years [Keckley 1994].

Capitation payment models, in which providers are willing to assume risk, allow payers to focus on "real costs," based on the specific benefits in insurance plans and historical utilization patterns. In addition, quality, ethical service providers who deliver focused treatment in a managed care environment can succeed without the characteristic distrust of payers that is so prevalent in the mental health care business environment.

Capitation payment models are not appropriate for many organizations because of the inherent financial risk involved. Some large, multiservice, multisite organizations, however, and others that are able to partner with agencies with complementary services, may find that capitation service contracts are advantageous. This is especially true for child welfare agencies that have invested significantly in community-based, brief service treatment models.

References

Keckley, P. H. (1994, May 6). *Resetting the stage.* Speech delivered to Family Service of America Conference, Houston, Texas.

Hazlitt, W. (1819). Quoted in Safire, L., & Safire, W. (1982). Good advice (p. 694). New York: Time Books.

4 CASE STUDIES

...chance favors only the mind that is prepared
—Louis Pasteur [1927]

Arizona Children's Home Association, Tucson, AZ
Fred Chaffee, M.S.W., Executive Director

The Arizona Children's Home Association (ACHA), one of the oldest agencies in the state, was founded in 1914 to provide statewide family foster care and adoption services, and to prevent neglected and abandoned children from being sent to California. In 1922, the agency established an orphanage. In the 1950s, ACHA opened group foster homes and began serving children referred by the courts. In the 1960s and 1970s, the agency took a number of steps toward becoming a full service, multisite agency. Family preservation services were launched in the 1980s. ACHA's residential program has been accredited by JCAHO for 30 years.

The Arizona Children's Home Association currently has a budget of $7.5 million, and employs 220 staff members statewide. With offices in 11 cities, it offers a full range of services, including outpatient, group homes, therapeutic foster care, adoption and special-needs adoption, residential treatment, and drug and alcohol inpatient services, and an employee assistance program. Its behavioral health care services include capitated intensive outpatient, in-home family therapy, and family preservation services.

ACHA first gained access to Medicaid funds in 1988; it began pursuing managed care in 1992. When asked how his agency decided to pursue managed care, Executive Director Fred Chaffee indicated that the state of Arizona had decided the issue for the agency by implementing a form of behavioral health managed care. As fate would have it, ACHA's board president happened to be the CEO of one of the largest HMOs in the area. The board president, along with other members of the board who are involved in health care, provided support and guidance as the agency moved in this new direction.

In addition to this preparation, Fred engaged experienced managed care consultants to help the staff implement new systems, including improvement of access to services, implementation of statistical and outcome measures, and establishment of a seamless network of services. The outpatient staff readily embraced the changes, while the residential staff were slow to accept them and were concerned about permanency issues.

Fred acknowledged that there were difficulties during the transition. First, the clinical staff had trouble making the transition from traditional ways of dealing with clients to viewing clients as customers who might actually know what they want from the therapeutic relationship. The slow transition to a seamless service system actually became a critical incident that threatened the viability of one managed care contract. The staff had expressed their commitment to provide seamless care; their actions, however, were contrary to the stated goal. Resolving the problem required a great deal of utilization monitoring and administrative resolve.

More recently, ACHA became involved in putting together a bid to become, in partnership with several other agencies, a for-profit managed care company that would manage all of the behavioral health care dollars for southern Arizona. If successful, the company would be responsible for the administration and allocation of $300,000 in benefits over the next five years.

The experience of putting together such a large entity has, in Fred's words, "changed the provider landscape in southern Arizona forever." Even if the bid is unsuccessful, a by-product of establishing this large entity has been the setting in place of the key elements of an integrated delivery system.

Fred foresees three possibilities for the future of managed

care. First, he predicts that managed care will be universally applied to the child welfare and juvenile justice system. Second, the MIS elements of managed care will help to identify service "exceptions"—those children requiring additional care—and those agencies that are less successful. Last, he believes that over time MCOs will become allies with child-serving in caring for the "deep end" children.

As the federal rules and regulations change, putting more dollars into block grants and giving power to the states with a concomitant cut in all other dollars available, Fred believes that the attractiveness to the public sector of increasingly effective management of the benefits and resource changes will grow exponentially.

Fred's advice to other CEOs is to embrace the positive aspects of managed care, and the improvement in the system that it will generated, and to deliberately pursue the opportunities it creates.

Bellefaire, Cleveland, OH
Sam Kellman, Ph.D., Executive Director

In 1868, Bellefaire was established by B'nai B'rith (a Jewish fraternal organization) as an orphanage to care for Jewish children. The agency's transition from orphanage to mental health center began in 1924 when Bellefaire hired a staff psychiatrist and began accepting children who had emotional problems or whose parents could not take care of them. By the end of the 1940s, Bellefaire had merged with the Jewish Children's Bureau and several additional child-caring institutions and made the transition to a mental health and child development agency. An on-grounds school became an integral part of the program in the 1950s. In the 1960s, Bellefaire was one of the first agencies to establish a secure cottage program and a day-treatment program. Bellefaire began promoting child development in the 1970s; in the early 1980s, it launched an in-home family preservation program.

Currently, Bellefaire has an annual budget of $17 million, and employs 300 staff members. Its 27 distinct programs and services cover the entire array of child welfare and children's mental health services and include community services such as day care, family guidance, community education, and a Big Brothers/Big Sisters program; traditional child welfare, outpatient therapy, and mental health services; and foster care residential and secure residential services.

The decision to pursue insurance contracts had its roots in the early 1980s, as Jewish communities throughout the nation found it difficult to afford the level of service provided by Bellefaire. This led to discussions by Bellefaire with insurance companies, and to contracts to provide services. By the late 1980s, insurance companies began limiting lengths of stay in mental health facilities and reducing mental health benefits, which led to further interaction between Bellefaire and the managed care firms. To date, these efforts have been largely successful.

Bellefaire Executive Director Sam Kellman indicated that developing an organizational structure that was responsive to the needs of managed care was the greatest challenge during the transition. He has learned that MCOs place great emphasis on justifying the continued need for service, and that, if an agency can demonstrate (1) continuing need and (2) reasonable benefit to the client, the MCOs are usually accommodating. Willingness to meet the justification needs of the MCOs in a timely fashion is one key to success. Putting this kind of customer-friendly system in place was another challenge for the staff. Sam recommends that agencies concentrate upon "high touch, not high tech" when pursuing exceptional customer service.

Sam Kellman is known for his keen insights and his ability to analyze public policy issues. Therefore, his concerns about the future of child welfare should be especially noted. He is not looking forward to the prospect of child welfare and children's mental health systems being absorbed by the managed care companies. His concern is that the nation is in the process of turning an entitlement into a categorical grant with fixed funding, an effort that he fears will result in health care rationing driven by funding, not by a national public policy debate to determine the direction of health care in our society. Ultimately, he foresees that people will be hurt by a system that is primarily concerned with cost. In particular, the "deep end" children served by child welfare agencies will suffer as money is diverted from their care to serve a broader segment of society. Sam's preference would be a public, single-payer system, where cost and quality would be evenly balanced. A further concern is that private companies, dependent upon potentially billions of dollars in public funding, will come to control the political process in order to protect their interests.

Brightside for Families and Children, West Springfield, MA
Peter Salerno, President and CEO
Cynthia Smith, M.S.W., Executive Director

Brightside was founded in the early 1870s by the Sisters of Providence to serve the health and welfare needs of immigrant families in western Massachusetts. In the mid-1870s, the Sisters constructed an orphanage to serve up to 100 children, and established a hospital and adoption program. In response to changes in the church and society in the 1960s, a residential program was established.

Brightside   first began to implement modern social work practices, including work with families, in the 1980s. Brightside established parent support programs, teen mother initiatives, and group homes. A crossroads was reached in 1989 when cuts in federal and state funding almost led to the closing of the residential campus. From this came a strategic planning effort that led to an emphasis on preventative services, a family-centered approach, and a renewed commitment to financial viability.

Currently, Brightside has a budget of $12 million and 360 employees. Its broad array of services include multisite outpatient and nonhospital inpatient services, an 80-bed residential campus, and a specialized program for sex offenders. According to Executive Director Cynthia Smith, two of Brightside's most innovative programs are an in-home service program for newborns exposed prenatally to drugs and their mothers, and a day-treatment program for mothers combined with day care for their children.

Brightside has implemented managed care throughout its range of programs, with the outpatient services as the backbone of the operation. Technically, Brightside serves as a PPO for 200,000 lives, and must compete with a number of other providers for clients. Its approach to this competition is to heavily market its services, and to quickly respond to the needs of payers and families 24 hour per day.

The ability to provide immediate access and implement computer technology were essential elements of Brightside's preparation for, and implementation of, managed care. According to Cynthia, Brightside was able to recognize early in the process that a computer network would aid Brightside's efforts to respond to the new demands of the marketplace. Other elements that have contributed to its success include a triage system, seamless services, and the establishment of service protocols and standards.

Some of Brightside's trustees had difficulty making the transition to managed care. One of the steps the Board took was to closely align the organization with the nearby Providence Hospital, thereby enhancing Brightside's status as a health care provider.

Staff members also had difficulty during the transitional period. The clinicians wanted to maintain their independence and traditional relationship with clients. One method of dealing with the resistance to therapeutic productivity was to make some of the therapists contract employees, and to pay them a set rate per hour of therapy. This approach allowed the therapists the flexibility of an independent contractor, while limiting Brightside's expenses. They are now expected to provide 24-26 billable hours of therapy per week, provide computerized client progress updates, and reduce time spent on activities such as individual staff supervision.

Brightside has faced and overcome a number of critical incidents since 1989. In 1991, Mental Health Management of America contracted with Brightside to provide step-down services. During this time, Brightside lost money, but nevertheless invested heavily in its computer system. Since then, Brightside has experienced some lean years, and sometimes employees have gone without pay raises. As of 1994, however, Brightside is again in the black and financially successful.

When asked what she foresees for child welfare systems over the next three to five years, Cynthia predicts that child welfare will ultimately become part of the health care system. She believes that child welfare agencies need to make some trade-offs between how agencies pursue their missions and what MCOs want in terms of performance and efficiency. Her advice to executives is to first have a firm grasp of their agencies' missions, values, and strategic plans. Furthermore, agencies will need to become clinically and financially astute. To prepare for managed care, agencies will need to measure and know their outcomes, provide a seamless system of services, and be culturally competent. Admissions processes must be designed to be responsive to crises, and agencies cannot maintain a waiting list. Executives will need to understand what the payers want, which MCOs are operating in their area, and the demographics of their market. Her final, and most succinct, advice to executives facing the prospect of managed care is to "just do it" by moving quickly to implement the necessary changes.

Children and Families of Iowa, Des Moines, IA
Donna Walgren, M.A., B.S.W., Executive Director

Children and Families of Iowa was founded in 1888 by a group of private citizens anxious to find homes for orphaned children. In 1898, the agency established a receiving home and continued to emphasize adoption. In the 1960s, the agency added specialized foster care, a family counseling program, and established two group homes for emotionally disturbed children. During the 1980s, Children and Families continued to expand throughout Iowa; it operated six group homes, along with a variety of foster care and family support programs. In the early 1990s, the agency merged with four others to broaden the range of care and treatment options it provides.

Today, Children and Families has a budget of $11 million and employs 440 full- and part-time staff members. Its comprehensive range of services include day care, parent education, tutoring, chemical dependency, family violence, family counseling and in-home support, family foster care, group care, and independent living. Children and Families currently provides behavioral health care services for 2,500 covered lives. In 1995, the number will increase to 10,000, and the agency will provide services throughout most of Iowa through its Circle of Care product.

Donna Walgren's interest in managed care began in 1984 when she was appointed to the Board of Blue Cross/Blue Shield of Iowa. More recently, a donor to both Children and Families and the local Mercy Hospital suggested that Mercy assist Children and Families to prepare for their 1994 JCAHO certification. This joint dialogue, combined with the agency's merger with a drug and alcohol treatment organization, put Children and Families in position to provide behavioral health care services. A letter of intent was signed between Mercy Hospital and Children and Families in 1993, and the staffs of the two organizations began meeting twice a week. This effort culminated in a partnership between the two organizations to develop a jointly owned §501(c)(3) corporation for behavioral health care services—the Circle of Care. Donna is quick to point out, however, that this is not a merger.

The reaction of staff and trustees to the managed care initiatives has been favorable. In particular, the therapeutic staff were largely thankful that someone was looking to safeguard the organization and their collective future. The directors were initially concerned that they might become part of a for-profit entity; the partnership with Mercy Hospital was therefore established as a nonprofit.

Donna has a hopeful vision of the impact of managed care over the next few years. She believes that managed care will close the gap between the quality of care received by private and public insurance clients, leading to the homogenization of the two systems of care. She further believes that the medical community will begin to have a greater appreciation for the services provided by child welfare agencies. While she foresees some danger during the transition years, she feels that behavioral health care will ultimately play an important role in promoting wellness and early intervention for children and families in crisis.

Her advice to other executives considering the transition to managed care is to influence events instead of being victimized by them. Change is not always negative, she is quick to stress, especially considering the weaknesses of and problems with the current child welfare system. She suggests that child welfare agencies should begin to focus on their clients' strengths, and to be respectful of both their clients and their customers. Further, she encourages CEOs to learn all they can about managed care, and to view it as an opportunity to create their agencies' destiny.

DePelchin Children's Center, Houston, TX
Robert E. Barker, M.S.W., President/CEO

DePelchin Children's Center was founded in 1892 as an orphanage. Like many orphanages established in the last century, it has gradually added to its array of services over the years. By the mid-1970s, the agency was providing teen pregnancy services, adoption services, family foster care, and emergency shelter services, and had established a large basic child welfare institution for school-aged "dependent and neglected" children. In 1978, two of the six campus cottages (a total of 22 beds) were converted into a residential treatment facility.

In 1981, a nine-bed hospital unit for children was established in a building that was once a campus clinic. At the time the hospital was developed, there were no psychiatric hospital beds for children in the county. DePelchin's entry into the world of medical insurance occurred when the hospital opened in 1981. One of the first contracts it signed was with Blue Cross for both hospital and residential treatment services. DePelchin's entry into the world of managed care, therefore, was more gradual and more evolutionary than that of most organizations.

Today, DePelchin provides a wide array of children's services, including crisis outpatient services, short-term outpatient mental health services, residential treatment, partial hospitalization services, treatment foster care, home-based therapy, psychiatric hospital services, post-adoption therapy, child abuse treatment services, teen parent services, and adoption services. Managed care services are primarily provided in outpatient therapy, partial hospitalization services, residential treatment and psychiatric hospital services.

During 1987, a major insurance company expressed interest in purchasing services from DePelchin for their HMO product. DePelchin began a relationship with this insurance company on a discounted fee-for-service basis, and, by mutual consent, converted the contract to a capitated contract in 1990. Since 1987, DePelchin has been providing all of the mental health services for this HMO's child and adolescent population (about 65,000 people). This experience opened the door to working with other managed care companies. DePelchin Children's Center currently has 24 managed care contracts.

Initially, DePelchin made few changes in how it provided services. Lengths of stay were not reassessed, costs were not closely examined, and staff did not receive special training in managed care service delivery. In 1990, the first year of the capitated contract, the agency lost approximately $125,000.

As a result of this experience, DePelchin began establishing systems to track treatment planning and lengths of stay, developing norms for programs, and training staff on the principles of managed care. Members of the board of directors also worked on planning. DePelchin's board and management were determined to maintain a balance between managed care services and services to children and families in the public sector. Once the balance was determined, it became apparent that to succeed under managed care, DePelchin would need to expand its outpatient mental health care service delivery capacity.

This expansion was accomplished in 1992, through a merger with Houston Child Guidance Center (the largest private, nonprofit, outpatient children's mental health organization in Houston). Houston Child Guidance Center provided services at five different locations in the greater Houston community. This merger has enabled DePelchin to enter into major managed care contracts, and to assure MCOs that it has sufficient outpatient and crisis intervention services to prevent unnecessary inpatient admissions.

For at least the first two years, services were more customer-focused for insured clients than for those referred by public agencies. Staff correctly pointed out that this dual system often meant better services for the private payers. For example, therapists tended to be available more often on weekends and evenings to meet with the parents of private-pay clients. Inasmuch as the public sector clients did not request the same flexible, customer-oriented approach, the organization was less likely to provide the extra services.

DePelchin's business office lacked the experience and competency to manage copayment collections and the required tracking with insurance companies to follow-up on claims that had not been paid or had been only partially paid. The result was a significant increase in insurance receivables, some of which were never collected and later had to be written off.

Many staff members, even after several years of experience and training, continue to wrestle with such issues as length of stay, utilization management, outside review, and decision making by managed care companies. One of the major challenges for DePelchin is undoing the training most clinicians receive in graduate programs, which frequently focuses on longer-term psychodynamic treatment. This runs counter to the realities of providing services under managed care, which emphasizes brevity of services.

Parents paying for care through their insurance policies (and possibly paying a deductible as well) usually feel more empowered than the parents of children served through public sector contracts. When agency services do not produce the desired results or critical incidents occur—such as a child receiving minor injuries during restraint—the threat of legal action by the former group of clients increases. As a result, DePelchin Children's Center has had to devote additional staff time to risk management processes.

Although DePelchin Children's Center has not had any judgments or damages assessed against it, one suit, filed and dismissed, took considerable staff time and more than two years to prepare for and defend.

To increase efficiency and effectiveness for the managed care and public sector populations it serves, DePelchin plans to strengthen and expand its crisis intervention and respite care services. It believes that these services work well for most children who would otherwise be hospitalized or placed in residential treatment.

DePelchin also plans to expand its research activities and is currently conducting a longitudinal study that will compare diagnosis to outcome in hospital, residential treatment, and partial hospitalization services. Within a year, crisis intervention services and outpatient services will be included in the research activities.

Kids Peace, Kids Peace, PA
John P. Peter, M.S.W., President/CEO

Founded 120 years ago, Kids Peace is one of the largest children's agencies in the United States. It employs 1,400 people, and has an annual budget of approximately $70 million. Close to 500 residential beds are in service at several sites, in addition to a 72-bed psychiatric hospital. The organization is multistate, and has a long history of serving both privately and publicly insured clients.

Kids Peace has provided residential services throughout its history; it was one of the first agencies to develop residential treatment programs nearly 30 years ago. Other mental health services were developed at about the same time.

Kids Peace is one of the few CWLA member agencies that provides psychiatric hospital services. The array of services provided include multilevels of residential programming (including group homes) and a variety of residential services of differing intensities and specialties. In addition, partial hospitalization, intensive family treatment, family preservation services, family development, and outpatient mental health services are provided.

In addition to its contracts with public child welfare agencies, Kids Peace also provide services through one or more managed care contracts. Currently, it has approximately 20 such contracts. During 1989 and 1990, its management recognized the need to expand the agency's referral and customer base, and to prepare for the future by gaining experience operating in aggressive managed care environments. As a result, Kids Peace studied the market and its needs. It began to identify key managed care organizations to target for contract negotiations. Securing these new contracts provided an opportunity to change the culture of the organization. Most of the contracts had specific requirements in terms of utilization management or clinical reports that required staff training in order to comply.

Major organizational change occurred in the development of improved customer and client satisfaction measurements. The staff was trained in various aspects of child, parent, and employer responsiveness, and in the expectations of specific managed care organizations. Dr. David Doty, Director of Professional Standards, indicated that major steps were taken by Kids Peace to address weaknesses in the "managed care readiness" aspects of its operations.

Staff initially expressed concern that Kids Peace would have to develop two systems of care—one for public agency children and another for the private market. There was concern that the brief treatment focus of managed care companies would not be compatible with the needs of public agency children. This issue was addressed by providing additional information and by expanding the array of available services. These services include components that address the long-term treatment needs of some public agency children, and the occasional private pay child whose insurance actually agrees to pay for longer treatment than specified by the contract.

Some staff members, especially those who had been with the organization a number of years, initially resisted the changes required to be responsive to the managed care market realities.

Through small group discussions, training opportunities, and actual experience with managed care cases, staff comfort with the new demands and expectations gradually increased. The availability of family development, family preservation, and outpatient services have increased staff treatment options, and have impressed MCOs with the commitment of Kids Peace to a less restrictive treatment philosophy.

David envisions Kids Peace converting some of their public-funded services to Medicaid-funded services. In most states, Medicaid will be managed more aggressively. This will result in minimizing the differences existing between the private pay and public pay markets. He recommends that organizations considering managed care contracts begin to gradually develop experience with managed care cases by signing a few contracts. They can then determine the expectations of the MCOs and attempt to make the initial organizational changes required to meet the contract expectations. He further recommends that organizations thoroughly assess their managed care readiness and develop strategic plans that address the long-term changes necessary for success under managed care.

Orchard Place, Des Moines, IA
Earl Kelly, Ph.D., CEO

In 1886, Orchard Place was established in Des Moines as an orphanage; it remained a basic child care institution until its board of directors decided in 1961 to convert it to a residential treatment center. In 1989, the organization became a Medicaid provider. Today, Orchard Place has a budget of more than $6 million and employs 160 individuals. The agency has 118 residential beds and a 50-child day treatment capacity.

Orchard Place has a reputation for providing excellent services to children and adolescents with emotional and behavioral problems. Its services include residential treatment, day treatment, outpatient mental health services, and delinquency prevention and treatment. A diagnostic/evaluation service guides the selection of the appropriate service for the youth.

Orchard Place has had several managed care contracts, and provided services on a "discounted" fee-for-service basis for several years. Residential treatment is most often the only service accessed by managed care companies. To increase the agency's responsiveness to managed care and the number of insurance companies willing to contract with it, CEO Earl Kelly decided that Orchard Place should be accredited by JCAHO. In addition, management believed that JCAHO accreditation would provide the basis for the systems changes needed to succeed as a Medicaid provider. In order to meet MCO requirements, Orchard Place is developing a brief intervention system for residential treatment, day treatment, and outpatient mental health services.

The decision to pursue managed care contracting was primarily the result of the state of Iowa's decision to contract out the Medicaid program to a single managed care organization. This organization was given the power to select residential treatment, day treatment, outpatient counseling services, and crisis intervention service providers. Earl states that as a result of the managed care Medicaid model implemented in Iowa, Orchard Place will become brief intervention, problem-focused, and mental health stabilization oriented in these targeted programs.

Orchard Place is in the process of training staff to understand the realities of providing services under managed care. The transition period will require review of the basic philosophies guiding current agency practice. The business office and utilization management functions of the organization will have to change to ensure that they adequately track clinical/utilization issues, unit costs, billing, and collection activities.

Prior to late 1994 and early 1995 (when the Medicaid program was contracted out to an managed care organization), Orchard Place primarily served public sector clients, providing only occasional services to managed care clients. Earl anticipates that most major organizational changes and staff/board adjustments will occur in 1995 and 1996, as the agency begins receiving most of its referrals through the managed care organization that holds the state Medicaid contract. Organizational changes will be required if Orchard Place is to successfully compete in a managed care environment while remaining committed to the its mission.

St. Joseph Children's Treatment Center, Dayton, OH
David Emenhiser, Ed.D., Executive Director

St. Joseph Children's Treatment Center was founded in 1849 as a Catholic children's aid society to serve children left orphaned after a cholera epidemic swept through southwest Ohio. After the Civil War, an orphanage was built to keep pace with the growing number of children in need. In the 1950s, the organization moved toward serving dependent and neglected children of all religious faiths and by the 1970s, began to focus upon the needs of abused children and became nonsectarian. By the early 1980s, St. Joseph's began providing mental health services and receiving Medicaid funding for its partial hospitalization program.

St. Joseph's current budget is $8 million; it employs 175 full-time staff members. Services include secure diagnostic and crisis stabilization, residential treatment, therapeutic foster care, group homes, partial hospitalization, independent living, outpatient, treatment preschool, in-home family preservation, in-school intensive outpatient, and an alternative school. The agency provides services in a number of sites throughout southwestern Ohio.

Montgomery County, Ohio (where Dayton is located) has been a managed care pilot for the state since 1988. All Medicaid-eligible clients receive their health care coverage from one of three HMOs in the area. St. Joseph's holds provider contracts with these managed care entities, and has been accepting referrals, primarily for outpatient and its various partial hospitalization programs. The agency has contracts with a number of MCOs.

Recently the state of Ohio announced the implementation of OhioCare, a managed care plan that extends health care for all Medicaid clients statewide. OhioCare will combine mental health and child welfare funding into a behavioral health care benefit. The state's request for a Medicaid waiver set the agenda for St. Joseph's move toward providing additional behavioral health care services. Its management team began attending state and national conferences on managed care, and bringing in national consultants to learn as much as possible about this new approach.

Based on this knowledge, St. Joseph's began to aggressively prepare for managed care. Some of the internal changes the agency made included establishing a unified admissions process, designing a customer service satisfaction survey directed at both parents and referral sources, acquiring a computer network, developing a secure diagnostic and crisis stabilization unit, and further expanding its array of services. Other steps included the appointment of a Director of Managed Care Planning and Implementation, participation in the CWLA Odyssey study to comprehensively track client outcomes, and establishment of satellite offices for outpatient services. St. Joseph's also embarked on a series of management team, board, therapeutic, and supervisory staff retreats to study the impact of managed care and begin to change the nature of its internal operations. Throughout the process of preparation and expansion, the board trustees have become educated about the implications of managed care and have included managed care objectives in the agency's strategic plan. A crucial element of the efforts has been St. Joseph's initiation of negotiations to establish regional and statewide provider networks.

References

Pasteur, L. (1927). Quoted in Bartlett, J. (1968). *Familiar quotations* (14th ed.) (p. 718). Boston: Little, Brown, and Company.

5 THE FUTURE

None of us knows what is ahead... The important thing is to use today wisely and well, and face tomorrow eagerly and cheerfully, and with the certainty that we shall be equal to what it brings.
—Channing Pollock [1943]

Managed care can be viewed either as an emerging threat to child welfare organizations, or as a promising reality that can contribute to positive organizational change. The requirements and expectations that managed care companies are placing on behavioral health care providers are the same as those that have already been imposed on America's private industries. For example, pressures from foreign auto manufacturers forced American auto manufacturers to produce better cars at competitive prices and to give customers choices. Therefore, relying on quality measurements, making efficient use of corporate resources such as factories, and building cars that met customer needs became essential to the survival of the American automobile industry.

The managed care industry is applying many of these same principles to the process of purchasing and delivering behavioral health care services. For the next few years, it will appear that the bulk of the managed care industry is concerned only with low prices and minimal service delivery. Managed care companies that plan to survive in the long term, however, will also need to be concerned about quality, as measured in terms of customer satisfaction. In this sense, the customers become both the users and the payers of services.

At the early stages of the process, managed care companies will clearly have the advantage. They control much of the process and hold most of the money. Currently, child welfare service providers lack verifiable research to refute the business strategies of many managed care organizations. These strategies often define corporate success in terms of keeping costs low enough to generate a reasonable profit for the MCO, keeping behavioral health care insurance costs for corporations lower than they should be, and providing the least amount of clinical services possible.

Eventually, however, the user and payer public will expect the managed care industry and the behavioral health care industry to deliver services that are affordable *and* effective. Just as the pressures and expectations placed on the American auto industry changed its way of operating, payers and users will change the face of managed care as they begin demanding funding for preventative and early intervention services. Many child welfare agency executives have been advocating for years for adequate funding for preventative and early intervention services, and the long-term savings in lives and dollars that these services can achieve. Various citizen alliance groups, hospitals, and other health care groups will become allies with child welfare agencies in advocating for adequate services under managed care.

The National Association of Children's Hospitals and Related Institutions (NACHRI), partially in response to the reality of managed care, and the need for some level of national health care reform, issued a position statement in October 1994 on the *Mental Health Needs of Infants, Children and Adolescents,* noting that

> Children who experience emotional, behavioral, mental, or addictive disorders, as well as children with developmental or learning disabilities, should have access to a broad continuum of traditional and nontraditional mental health services, ranging from early intervention to inpatient hospitalization. According to their clinical needs, children should also have access to multidisciplinary specialists trained to meet the unique emotional and behavioral needs of children. [NACHRI 1994]

The position paper also included a statement affirming the need for services that are family focused, culturally competent and provided in community-based, least restrictive environments. It recommended that community service delivery systems be collaborative in nature, easily accessible, and involve child-serving organizations that represent the mental health, child welfare, education, juvenile justice, and health care systems. As essential providers of mental health services to children and families, institutions and individuals with expertise in child maltreatment should be included in all mental health service delivery systems.

The position taken by NACHRI is consistent with what has been stated in previous chapters of this publication. It supports the idea that appropriate mental health services for children and families can result in considerable cost savings. Early intervention with at-risk children and families can prevent expensive treatment of both mental and physical disorders, and reduce the need for costly child welfare and criminal justice interventions. Furthermore, delivery systems that incorporate an affordable, easily accessible continuum of care can realize savings by preventing serious disorders through the use of relatively less expensive treatments.

The Impact of Managed Care on Child Welfare Agencies

As managed care continues to evolve—and as it becomes the predominant service delivery model—child welfare agencies should anticipate a range of challenges arising in the future. These challenges (detailed below) will create new opportunities to redesign organizational structures, service systems, human resource management systems, and the technological aspects of organizations. They will also lead to new ways for CEOs to manage resources, work with boards, and compete effectively with the for-profit sector. These challenges are likely to include:

- **Shifts in service delivery philosophies.** In the future, child welfare agencies can expect to encounter service delivery philosophies that are consistent with at-risk arrangements, including (1) the provision of a full and creative array of services, and multiple levels of care that reflect different degrees of intensity; (2) an emphasis on least restrictive services; (3) the valuing of quick and effective diagnostic and treatment processes; (4) the delivery of care that is oriented toward quality outcomes; and (5) highly individualized treatment planning.

- **Increased emphasis on prevention and early intervention services.** Given current trends, it is likely that even greater emphasis will be placed on wellness and preventive modes of intervention—what some have called *pre-intervention.* Prevention and early intervention are certain to be continuing points of interest for managed care companies. There may be a variety of ways in which these services are provided, however, and child welfare agencies will need to explore creative ways to provide these services, if not directly, then through advocacy or other means.

- **Growth in competition.** If current indicators hold true, large, for-profit providers will continue to enter the marketplace, especially as managed care grows and becomes more entrenched. Frequently, these providers, by virtue of their size and financial resources, will have substantial clout and opportunities to secure contracts. They will create a new environment of competition for the nonprofit sector.

- **Service provider integration and collaboration.** As managed care continues to grow, it is likely that more will be expected of service providers in terms of working together and coordinating resources and services. Collaboration—which already exists to varying degrees among child welfare service providers, will be crucial to effective participation in managed care arrangements. Expectations of integration and collaboration will demand increased flexibility and teamwork, and the ability to engage in group decision-making.

- **Service array, accessibility, and availability.** Increasingly, managed care organizations will require agencies to offer services that are geographically accessible, easily available, and provided at convenient hours for patients/clients. Clients will expect to be able to obtain routine appointments within a relatively short, defined period, and immediate emergency appointments. Child welfare services will be seen as a part of a full service array that meets the type and level of service appropriate to patient/client need.

- **Heightened accountability**. The use of outcome studies is certainly not unique to managed care, but the two have become inextricably linked. Outcome measurement is likely to become the primary means of managing resources. Accountability and the ability to show effectiveness of service delivery will become critical. Increasingly, "bang for buck" will be crucial in selecting the providers.

  Current expectations that providers be able to measure, demonstrate, and report effective and efficient outcomes are likely to continue. Service providers will be required to specify performance measures that help define what works, including measures of adherence to clinical criteria, patient satisfaction, and relapse/recidivism rates, and of the number, frequency, and outcomes of appeals related to treatment decisions. Patient satisfaction will continue to be highly important to MCOs but simple satisfaction surveys will not be viewed, in and of themselves, as credible indicators of therapeutic benefit.

- **Emphasis on value**. The focus on purchasing value will likely remain and increase as a critical managed care concept. Value, like outcome, will become a key ingredient in managed care. As Boland [1993] points out, "Quality will be used more as a positioning strategy by providers and as a score card by customers."

- **Sound management information systems**. A sound management information system that permits an agency to generate basic demographic and clinical information, facilitate utilization reviews, and assess client satisfaction and outcomes will be of continuing and growing importance. The techno-logical ability to collect, manage, and produce data will be essential to effective participation in managed care arrange-ments.

- **Financial and cost analysis capabilities.** Child welfare agencies must be able to determine how they can be truly competitive, and evaluate the extent to which they can accept non-fee-for-service reimbursement based upon a risk-sharing arrangement. In order to effectively participate in managed care systems, agencies will need to be able to assess the extent to which they can effectively engage in capitation and other managed care fiscal contracts.

Developing Partnerships with Purchasers of Services

Partnerships between payers of services and providers of ser-vices are the wave of the future. As they occur, compromise will be necessary in order to develop "win-win" scenarios for the providers of behavioral health care services and the purchasers of those services. The move toward partnership models will be the only way managed care will work in terms of the balance among the competing interests in cost management, quality, and freedom of choice.

Large employers are taking an increasingly active role in directing negotiations with service providers to obtain the spe-cific services they believe are necessary for their employees. Third-party administrators may manage the contract and the claims payment process, but employer representatives help design the service menu and meet often with service providers to assure contract compliance and to review quality reports, proof of treatment, and cost effectiveness.

For example, DePelchin Children's Center in Houston re-cently finalized contracts with two health care corporations to provide all of the behavioral health care services for children and adolescents enrolled in their insurance plans. The health care organizations met with representatives of DePelchin to determine the specific services provided by the agency that would be made available to the employees of their organizations. Agreement was also reached concerning the process for review of cases requiring prolonged and expensive services.

Development of Alliances

Managed care organizations will increasingly purchase most of their services from large provider organizations or alliances of providers. This will be true for both private insurance and Medicaid managed care products.

It is more efficient for managed care organizations to contract with a few large service providers or alliances and to track quality, utilization, and cost than to deal with many small providers. By definition, there are winners and losers under managed care. When some service providers are designated as preferred or given exclusive contracts to provide services, others are excluded and therefore, lose.

Private, nonprofit behavioral health care service providers must decide with whom to align themselves before choice is no longer an option. It may be that some large providers with a broad array of outpatient and inpatient services for children and adolescents can secure a sufficient number of contracts without forming alliances with other providers. In some markets, however, MCOs will only seek out providers or alliances of providers that provide adult, child, and adolescent behavioral health care services.

In most cases—and especially under Medicaid—MCOs contracting with providers for behavioral health care services will not require the service providers to be in alliance with medical/surgical hospitals and primary care physicians. In some private insurance managed care, however, there is an growing trend for capitated plans to require broad alliances that include behavioral health care and medical/surgical service providers. The MCOs assume that these type of alliances will provide the desired coordination and continuity of care.

The alliance developed by Child and Family Services of Iowa and Mercy Hospital in Des Moines, Iowa, is an example of a partnership that allowed a children's agency, as an alliance member, to enter into managed care contracts that it probably would not have if it had sought the contracts alone. In most situations, alliance partners need the services and reputation of the partner in order to access contracts. Such alliances also benefit adult behavioral health care and medical/surgical service providers by eliminating the need for them to develop competitive children and adolescent behavioral health services in order to access managed care contracts that require medical and behavioral health care services.

Managed Care Organizations: Will Only a Few Survive?

As the managed care revolution continues, it is becoming clear that the managed health care industry will soon be dominated by a small number of companies that will likely be operational in most states. Because of their dominance and financial reserves, these companies will have the power to play major roles in determining the types of behavioral health care services that will be purchased. This will be true for both private insurance and Medicaid plans. It is critical that the child welfare (behavioral health care) field be effectively organized and capable of advocating for appropriate services in the managed care plans.

A focus on quality and appropriate service utilization, and proof through research of effectiveness and efficiency, will be critical if the child welfare industry as we now know it is to survive under managed care. Quality will become increasingly important to payers, but at the same time, it will have to be cost effective. Research findings will begin to prove that overly restrictive delivery systems demanded by some payers will result in poor outcome and increased expenditures later on. Unless research findings are easily understood and produced by many behavioral health care service providers, employers or government agencies (in the case of Medicaid), payers will not give attention to the results.

All major players—governments, employers, managed care organizations, and service providers—have a stake in achieving the appropriate balance of cost containment and quality service provision. In order to control costs, access to the relatively more expensive services must be controlled. Too much control, however, may result in poor quality and high costs later on. Providers will have to be organized effectively in order to convince payers and customers of the importance of long-term results and the increased cost associated with services required in the future in overly aggressively managed plans.

Redesigning Organizations

Agency CEOs have the opportunity to use the unique challenges of the managed care environment to redesign their organizations. Boards of directors should show their support for outcome studies by helping to raise funds to underwrite such research. Staff should develop, support, and participate in the work required to have successful outcome studies. The outcome studies used will need to be of such quality that the results will be acceptable to employers, users of services, and MCOs. Child welfare organizations should collect their own data, change programs as needed because of the data, and communicate their findings to the managed care companies. In addition, efforts to collaborate in research with similar organizations should occur.

Redesigning Delivery Systems

Financial pressures that are being created by the managed care environment provide opportunities to develop less costly, less restrictive services. Boards and staffs that in the past have resisted diversification may now be willing to reexamine their long-held beliefs about the almost sacred nature of expensive service modalities that are frequently not supported by research. Interestingly, as managed care has significantly reduced the number of psychiatric hospital admissions and days per admission, there have been no reports of increases in either injuries or deaths of mentally ill individuals because of changes in service delivery. Assuming that additional child welfare organizations add to their array of services and dramatically reduce the length of stay in residential treatment, it is possible that the same results will occur.

Redesigning Human Resource Management Systems

The surplus of behavioral health care practitioners will continue to be a problem. The high no-show rate in many mental health outpatient clinics is a sign that our field has many practitioners who cannot effectively engage people. Just as for-profit providers have had to address this issue, so will nonprofit providers who hope to survive under managed care.

One obstacle to achieving a financially viable operation in the current traditional payer environment is the fixed nature of clinical service expenses, specifically personnel costs associated with maintaining a core of full-time clinicians who are compensated for their availability (40 hours per week), rather than their productivity (hours of direct service). Under the traditional model, when demand for services drops, income drops below expenses and a deficit is created. Conversely, when demand grows, staff feel burdened by increased demands upon their time without increased compensation.

One model, already successfully implemented by some behavioral health care organizations, is to provide office space for licensed clinicians to use in providing services to managed care clients. The organization's name is on the door and the clinician is actually an employee who is paid for each hour of production at a rate that allows appropriate revenue retention for the organization. A minimum productivity level is established to maintain employee status as full-time and an hourly rate is established for each hour of production. As the number of hours of production vary each month, the actual amount of pay is increased or decreased. Under this model, expenses relate directly to performance.

This trend in managed service delivery meets two important goals: (1) it ties together fluctuations in income and expenses, and (2) it rewards staff members for improvements in time management and increased customer satisfaction.

Redesigning Technological Aspects of the Organization

CEOs should use the opportunities associated with the arrival of managed care to strategically invest their agencies' resources in information systems, payer research, clinical program development, and strategic planning. Staff performance, in terms of the quality and quantity of work produced, can be measured effectively with available management information systems. As the transition to management information systems occurs, nonprofit child welfare agencies will need to reassess the traditional supervisory structures that they currently have in place. Admittedly, this is difficult to do, but the successful organizations of the future will be those that give increased responsibility to individual staff members, provide minimal supervision, have management information systems in place to measure performance, and then hold staff accountable for the results.

This new model will empower staff, save money, and produce the most effective services. In his book *The Fifth Discipline*, Senge [1990] describes this shift from intense supervision to personal accountability as a burden-lifting process, which can enable staff to achieve personal mastery. Senge describes staff with a high level of personal mastery as having a special sense of purpose that lies behind their vision and goals. They see current reality as an ally rather than an enemy. They have learned how to perceive and work with forces of change rather than resist those changes. People with personal mastery, according to Senge, take responsibility for their own learning needs and seek "experts" out in the organization when they need help, instead of having regular, traditional supervisory sessions with their supervisor.

One could argue that work environments that create this type of employee should be put into place whether or not managed care exists. This is true, but human nature in organizations is such that it frequently takes major pressures or events to cause such fundamental structural change.

The authors have observed a number of child welfare agencies that continue to have staff/supervisory models that involve several hours of individual and team supervision for clinical staff every week. In these agencies, clinicians seldom use as much as 50% of their available hours in direct clinical work. Caseloads often are low and the cost to deliver services is higher than it needs to be. In the managed care environment, these same organizations will be competing with organizations that expect 60% to 70% of a clinician's time to be spent directly providing clinical services.

Master's level and Ph.D. level staff should be provided with productivity standards and given the opportunity to decide their own learning needs within established parameters. This assumes that the quality of their work remains high. The increased productivity because of this new philosophy will help the organization become efficient.

Redesigning Resource Management

Most child welfare agencies hold considerable assets in properties and buildings. As donated funds become increasingly difficult to secure, and public and private payers require services other than institutional services for children, decisions will have to be made in terms of redeploying real property assets. In many cases, real property assets will need to be converted to provide outpatient office space, day treatment program space, and funds for the endowment to provide services for children and families that fall through the safety net.

Considerable leadership and time will be required of CEOs in convincing boards of the need to make these changes, particularly with respect to selling land that in many cases has been held by the organization for generations. Kay Dobleman, Executive Director of the Brown Foundation in Houston, Texas, has stated that one of the major questions she asks of residential care providers with major land holdings is whether they need all of the land for programs. If the answer is no, she then asks if plans have been developed to sell some of the land, and the funds put to use in supporting the mission of the organization [Dobleman 1994]. Many CEOs will likely be spending considerable time addressing real property issues over the next few years.

Redesigning Board Management

A number of issues will probably affect how boards of directors and CEOs work together in the new environment of managed care. Boards will have to consider and be willing to authorize participation in at-risk contracts with managed care companies.

They will have to be willing to authorize management to respond quickly, often between board meetings, to negotiate contracts, and to make the major business decisions typical in corporate models of governance. There will not be time to endlessly process information and decisions at board meetings. For their part, CEOs will need to provide leadership to their boards in assessing opportunities for alliances and networks to participate in and potential candidates for merger.

CEOs will be at increased risk in terms of making decisions that could result in significant financial losses to their organizations, or in choosing partners who, because of poor quality, may pull their organizations into lawsuits. In this new environment, CEOs should consider seeking contractual relationships with their boards that will provide some protection for the career risks associated with the difficult judgments and decisions that will have to be made.

CEOs will need to educate their board members concerning the major change issues in behavioral health care service provision, and the need for organizations to discontinue some services and add others more relevant for today's payer environment. Because private and publicly funded managed care plans will frequently limit services to some clients, and exclude some children and families entirely from coverage, CEOs and board members will need to work closely together to raise private contributions and establish or enlarge endowment funds. These funds will be required for the children underserved in managed care plans or ineligible for services in public and private managed care plans.

Preparing for Increased Competition from For-Profits

The 1993 annual survey of the membership of the National Association of Psychiatric Health Systems (NAPHS) revealed that, in terms of residential treatment, 43% of all admissions were paid by Medicaid, Champus, or other governmental units. Approximately two-thirds of NAPHS's members are for-profit service providers who operate hospitals, residential and day treatment facilities, and in some cases, outpatient behavioral health care services [NAPHS 1994]. As Medicaid increasingly moves under managed care, and for-profit companies secure some of those managed care contracts, many for-profit providers will be directly competing with nonprofit agencies. In order to survive, the nonprofit sector will have to adopt many of the practices of the successful, ethical for-profit providers, including measuring quality, appropriately rewarding special producers within the organization, and never losing sight of the importance of achieving financial success. In addition, most successful for-profit organizations take quick corrective action when some current services need to be changed or discontinued and others added.

Summary

Management expert Peter Drucker states that a primary reason many nonprofits are unsuccessful is that they focus on needs instead of results. "Unfortunately," according to Drucker, "a great many nonprofits still believe that the way to get money is to hawk needs. But the American public gives for results" [Drucker 1991].

Based on Drucker's analysis, and the experiences of many child welfare organizations attempting to compete under managed care in the mid-1990s, nonprofit child welfare agencies are facing the same problems that have challenged business organizations. If nonprofit organizations are to thrive, their executive directors and boards must always be aware of the importance of focusing on productivity and performance issues. This is often a major challenge because direct service personnel (and often their supervisors) frequently focus on process rather than productivity. For example, clinical staff often focus on treatment modalities rather than trying to determine which treatment methods produce the most cost effective results. This can result in providing a client with a complex and expensive treatment, when a less costly treatment would work just as well. Managed care companies are fiscally motivated to seek out the less costly treatment modalities. Providers must do likewise to survive.

References

Boland, P. (1993), Market overview and delivery system dynamics. In P. Boland (Ed.), *Making managed health care work* (p. 12). Rockville, MD: Aspen.

Dobleman, K. (1994, September 9). Executive Director, Brown Foundation, Houston, Texas. Personal Communication.

Drucker, P. (1991, March–April). Nonprofits must counter attack on sector. *Nonprofit World*, p. 38.

National Association of Children's Hospitals and Related Institutions (NACHRI). (1994, October). *Position statement on the mental health needs of infants, children and adolescents*. Alexandria, VA: Author.

National Association of Psychiatric Health Systems (NAPHS). (1994, Fall). Annual survey results. Washington, DC: Author.

Pollock, C. (1943). Quoted in Safire, L., & Safire, W. (1982). *Good advice* (p. 132). New York: Time Books.

Senge, P. (1990). *The fifth discipline: Mastering the five practices of the learning organization* (pp. 143–145). New York: Doubleday.

Appendix A   GLOSSARY

Capitation—A managed care reimbursement mechanism; when payment is by capitation, a provider receives a fixed per capita (literally by the head) payment in exchange for furnishing all or part of the services provided to each person the health plan covers.

Cost Sharing—Health care costs the consumer pays out-of-pocket. Cost sharing may take a number of forms:

- *Deductibles*: A flat dollar amount that the individual pays before any benefits are paid (for example, $100).

- *Co-insurance*: A percentage of covered charges that the benefit plan pays (for example, 80%); the consumer is responsible for the remainder.

- *Copayments*: A flat dollar amount that an individual pays directly to a provider at the time that services are provided (for example, $5).

Cost Containment—The primary objective of managed care, even when its proponents say quality of care is uppermost; usually involves limiting reimbursement and controlling the use of service.

Fee for Service—Payment made to the provider at the time each service is provided. Fee-for-service payment is the opposite of capitation; it is generally not a managed care concept.

Forms of Managed Care—In the alphabet soup of ways that managed care can be provided, acronyms include:

- *EPO*: exclusive provider organization.

- *HIO*: health insuring organization.

- *HMO*: health maintenance organization.

97

- *IPA*: independent practice association.

- *IPO*: independent practitioner organization.

- *PCCM*: primary care case management.

- *PHP*: prepaid health plan.

- *PPO*: preferred provider organization.

Freedom of Choice—The requirement under Medicaid that eligible individuals be able to choose their service providers. To require participation in a managed care program, a state must obtain a freedom-of-choice waiver from HCFA.

HCFA—The Health Care Financing Administration, located within the U.S. Department of Health and Human Services; oversees Medicaid and Medicare.

Insurance Reform—Changes expected under any health care reform package, including those involving managed care, to make health insurance more available to consumers. This may include changes in such current practices as "exclusion for preexisting conditions" (denying insurance coverage to people already ill), "cherry picking" (charging healthy young people significantly lower rates), and "experience rating" (raising rates on the basis of a person's health history or occupation).

Medicaid Managed Care—A system of delivering care to individuals enrolled in Medicaid through contracted HIOs, HMOs, PHPs, and PCCM programs.

Network—The group of identified health care service providers to which a managed care plan directs patients/clients.

Risk—In managed care, the chance of not being fully reimbursed for services provided. Upon accepting the capitated amount from the managed care company, the provider is at risk that actual expenses may be greater than that amount.

Risk Adjustment—A process intended to compensate health care plans for the cost of enrolling high-risk individuals. Health alliances would contribute additional funds for some individuals to reflect the level of risk assumed.

Single Payer—An approach to health care reform in which the government is the payer for all health care.

Single Point of Entry—A key characteristic of managed care; individuals gain access to services through a primary health care provider who decides what additional services are needed.

Utilization Management—A system of reviewing and approving care that is characteristic of managed care; can include such activities as precertification (approval prior to delivery of services), concurrent review (review of service needs and service level while services are being delivered) and oversight of changes in level of care (periodic review of needed level of services).

Appendix B   SAMPLES

Sample Letter

Dear _____ :

St. Joseph Children's Treatment Center is a nondenominational, multiservice mental health agency. We serve children from age three to age 21, and their families. With the coming of OhioCare, we are interested in expanding our relationship with health care providers and insurers. I would like to meet with you, or your designee, to discuss the quality of our care and treatment, and the avenues of partnership. Please give me a call, and/or alert your executive secretary that Fred Sinay, our Director of Managed Care Planning and Implementation, will be calling in the next two weeks for an appointment.

Attached is a brief description of our plans and services.

Thank you for your time and attention.

Sincerely,

David Emenhiser, Ed.D.
Executive Director

Sample Attachment

Positioning for OhioCare Implementation

St. Joseph's has the courage, the foresight, and the expertise required to serve the future needs of children. We are also positioned to provide quality services at a competitive price.

For many years, St. Joseph's has been among the leaders in delivering children's mental health services, at costs below those of private providers and mental health centers. We have successfully negotiated service contracts that have kept the price of services at acceptable levels; we currently have several contracts with private insurers and HMOs.

By all major benchmarks, we have successfully grown to a large nonprofit organization.

- Our *Service* to the community is well-documented as one of the best in Ohio. We serve children from 45 counties in this state, and from as far away as Washington, D.C., and Arizona.

- Our *Commitment* to children has been demonstrated through 150 years of service and caring.

- Our *Client/Provider Satisfaction* surveys consistently rate our services as excellent.

- Our *Financial Strength* has allowed us to grow into the largest private mental health care provider in the area. Furthermore, we own all of our buildings and have an endowment.

- Our *Quality of Care and Treatment* is reflected in our Council on Accreditation certification, and our licensure from both the Ohio Department of Human Services and the Ohio Department of Mental Health.

Behind the improved services, client satisfaction, and financial success is the continuum of programs we offer at St. Joseph's. These programs provide care for children from age three to age 21. They include:

- A *Treatment Preschool* for three- to six-year-olds.

- A *Residential Treatment Program* for 48 boys and girls.

- A *Partial Hospitalization Program*.

- An *Alternative to School Program* for children suspended or expelled from regular schools.

- A *Special Treatment Foster Care Program* throughout southwest Ohio.

- An *Adoption Save Program* that focuses on providing therapy to adopted children and their families who are in danger of experiencing a failed adoption.

- A *Family Preservation Program.*

- *Outpatient Services.*

- *Short-Term Crisis Stabilization Services.*

In addition, our peer and utilization review programs continue to focus on appropriate lengths of stay, thus realizing substantial savings for our referral agencies. A new MIS/Client data base was installed within the past year. This has streamlined our billing process and improved the quality of data we provide to funders.

St. Joseph Children's Treatment Center has long understood the critical role managed care is destined to play in future health care reform. In anticipation of health care reform and the demand for accessible, competitive, delivery of quality service, we have experienced remarkable growth and still managed costs and utilization.

ABOUT THE AUTHORS

Robert E. Barker holds an M.S.W. from the University of Southern California and has been an administrator of human service organizations for more than 25 years. For the past 15 years, he has served as President and Chief Executive Officer of DePelchin Children's Center in Houston, Texas. DePelchin Children's Center is a 102-year-old, nonprofit children's mental health and child welfare organization, serving more than 19,000 individuals annually with a budget of approximately $16 million. DePelchin has provided services to managed care organizations since the mid-1980s and has had capitated payment contracts since 1990. Mr. Barker has consulted to private and public nonprofit organizations concerning management, board/staff issues, strategic planning, managed care, and accreditation.

Madelyn DeWoody is Associate Director for Planning, Training, and Evaluation for the Massachusetts Society for the Prevention of Cruelty to Children. She formerly served as General Counsel and Director of Child Welfare Services for the Child Welfare League of America in Washington, D.C. She is an attorney with a J.D. from the University of Houston and an LL.M. from Georgetown University Law Center, a social worker with an M.S.W. from Louisiana State University, and a public health practitioner with an M.P.H. from the University of North Carolina at Chapel Hill. Her work has focused on program development and financing in the area of child welfare, with particular emphasis on the health, mental health, and developmental needs of at-risk children and their families. She has written extensively on financing strategies for child welfare services, legal issues that impact child welfare policy and practice, and health care reform.

David Emenhiser, Ed.D., was appointed Executive Director of St. Joseph Children's Treatment Center on December 1, 1992.

Due to the trustees' commitment and the staff's dedication, St. Joseph has recently nearly tripled in size and capacity. Before coming to the agency, Dr. Emenhiser was Executive Director of The Villages of Indiana, Inc., which serves abused, neglected, and abandoned children throughout the state of Indiana. During his tenure with The Villages, it quintupled in size and income. Dr. Emenhiser holds a doctorate in Adult Development and Education and two master's degrees from Indiana University. He was appointed to the Board of the National Mental Health Association in the spring of 1993 and serves on its Managed Care Advisory Committee. In the spring of 1994, he was appointed to the International Child Welfare Technical Assistance Committee and in the fall of 1994, to the Managed Care Task Force of the Child Welfare League of America.